Personal Reading

HOW TO MATCH CHILDREN TO BOOKS

Rona F. Flippo
University of Massachusetts Boston

D1712492

Heinemann
Portsmouth, NH

Heinemann
A division of Reed Elsevier Inc.
361 Hanover Street
Portsmouth, NH 03801–3912
www.heinemann.com

Offices and agents throughout the world

Portions of this book have been previously published (and subsequently revised) in *Reading for Success in Elementary Schools* by Earl H. Cheek, Jr., Rona F. Flippo, and Jimmy D. Lindsey. Copyright © 1997. Published by McGraw-Hill.

The author and publisher wish to thank those who have generously given permission to reprint borrowed material:

Figures 1–4, 2–3, 8–1 and Appendices C–2, C–5, and D–1 from *Assessing Readers: Qualitative Diagnosis and Instruction* by Rona F. Flippo. Copyright © 2003 by Rona F. Flippo. Published by Heinemann, a division of Reed Elsevier, Inc., Portsmouth, NH. All rights reserved.

Figure 8–2 and Appendix D–2 from *How to Help Grow a Reader* by Rona F. Flippo. Copyright © 1982 by Rona F. Flippo. Published by Metro Atlanta/Georgia University Chapter of Phi Delta Kappa.

Library of Congress Cataloging-in-Publication Data
Flippo, Rona F.
    Personal reading : how to match children to books / Rona F. Flippo.
      p.   cm.
    Includes bibliographical references.
    ISBN 0-325-00667-9 (alk. paper)
    1. Children—Books and reading.   2. Reading (Elementary).   3. Guided reading.
  4. Activity programs in education.   I. Title.
Z1037.A1F59   2005
028.5′5—dc22   2005016344

Editor: Lois Bridges
Production service: Denise Botelho
Production coordinator: Sonja S. Chapman
Cover design: Night & Day Design
Compositor: Publishers' Design and Production Services, Inc.
Manufacturing: Jamie Carter

Printed in the United States of America on acid-free paper
09   08   07   06   05   VP   1   2   3   4   5

Elena and Zoe as they happily anticipate a favorite book

Contents

Introduction

One of the more important goals of developing children's reading is to develop their pursuit of and interest in reading independently, for personal satisfaction of their motivations and needs, as well as for pleasure. This book discusses the importance of developing the personal reading of each child in your classroom, and especially on how to meet the individual motivations and interests of each student and how to help each of them develop aspects of their personal reading. Matching children's diverse interests and motivations to books that will satisfy them is important to the development of their personal reading. This is a very different emphasis than the more common one of matching preselected books to children. Six purposes of personal reading are discussed: (1) current interests, (2) new and developing interests, (3) recreation, (4) academic interests, (5) practical purposes, and (6) pleasure.

Tools and procedures for developing each aspect of personal reading are provided at appropriate places throughout the book. These include attitude/feelings and perception questions; interest inventories and questions; reflection questions to help teachers work students' interests into the classroom curriculum; sustained silent reading (SSR) procedures; reading aloud to your students and sharing good literature with them; and questions to help guide your selection of reading materials using academic interests, children's prior knowledge, genre immersion, and the sharing of personal reading. Additionally, Try It Out activities are provided at the end of each chapter and at the end of the book. These activities have been designed to engage your students and keep them actively interested in developing their personal reading.

Parents, family and community life play a major role in children's attitudes about personal reading and in children's opportunities for personal reading. Parents and family are discussed and suggestions are made to include them in efforts to promote and continue children's personal reading at home and in the child's larger community life. Likewise, culture and sociocultural influences affect children's personal reading development, choices, and interests. Suggestions are made about how to use these choices and interests to promote the development of all students' personal reading.

This book also includes lists of professional references and resources that can facilitate teachers' efforts to find children's literature especially for their students. This literature can include "good taste" and "good literature" choices that children find particularly interesting or relevant for their individual interests, needs, and desires.

Main Ideas

- Personal reading is more than recreational reading.
- Current individual interests can be pursued and developed through personal reading.
- New and developing interests can be enhanced through personal reading.
- Personal reading can be for recreational purposes.
- Personal reading can be used to develop academic interests.
- Reading to enhance literary appreciation can be accomplished through personal reading.
- Personal reading can occur for practical purposes.
- Reading for pleasure is an important aspect of personal reading.
- Personal reading involves self-motivation and self-selection.
- Students' culture, community, and family all have an impact on students' personal reading.
- The aesthetic stance and individual desires are important to readers' personal reading enjoyment and involvement.
- The efferent stance is the stance readers take when they focus on the information to be learned from the text and then, ideally, find information they can use and relate to in the reading selection.
- Personal reading must never be pushed or forced on students by anyone.
- Personal reading development can be promoted by the classroom teacher's understandings and the many opportunities provided for students to read inside and outside the classroom.

Understanding Personal Reading

What is personal reading? Many would define it as recreational reading or the reading we do for our own pleasure. I agree with this definition but believe that personal reading includes much more. My definition of personal reading also includes individual pursuits of interests (current, developing, and academic) and individual pursuits for practical purposes. It really is using reading for one's own pleasure, interests, motivations, purposes, and needs. Figure 1–1 displays this concept of personal reading. As you know, all these aspects are influenced tremendously by each individual's culture, community, family, and personal needs and desires.

Reflection Activity 1.1
What do you believe personal reading involves? How does your idea of "personal reading" fit into your thoughts about the reading process, your role as a teacher, and the development of learners' literacy?

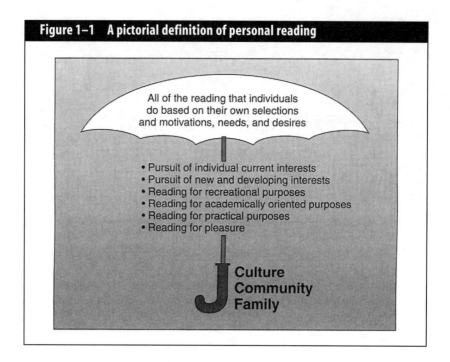

Figure 1–1 A pictorial definition of personal reading

All of the reading that individuals do based on their own selections and motivations, needs, and desires

- Pursuit of individual current interests
- Pursuit of new and developing interests
- Reading for recreational purposes
- Reading for academically oriented purposes
- Reading for practical purposes
- Reading for pleasure

Culture
Community
Family

Enhancing Reading Opportunities

A really important part of the classroom teacher's role is to help develop the personal reading of his or her students. Teachers can do this by enhancing reading opportunities. This means using every opportunity to foster the development of personal reading, for all children, and to plan instruction and learning opportunities that allow for the continued development of personal reading interests, habits, motivation, and selection. As illustrated in the personal reading umbrella in Figure 1–1, self-motivation and self-selection are fundamental. Self-motivation, of course, refers to motivation that comes from within. Self-selection refers to one's own personal choosing. The research and literature support the importance of self-motivation in all aspects of reading (e.g., Cramer and Castle 1994; Gambrell 2001; Guthrie 1994; Guthrie and Wigfield 1997; and Pressley et al. 2003).

Additionally, the classroom teacher must understand the importance of each individual's experiences, background, culture, and family/community influences. Because students are diverse and unique individuals, each student may develop different meanings, insights, and understandings from any piece of literature. It is critical for teachers to understand and respect these unique and often diverse individual meanings. The transactional theory of reading and writing (Rosenblatt 1978, 1989) supports the idea that the meaning a reader brings to text and the meaning that the writer intended is often reconstructed into a new, developed meaning as the reader creates and makes meaning as he or she reads. Reading is a very personal experience during which readers connect the story they are reading to their own lives and to their own personal experiences with literature. They don't search for the author's "correct message," but instead create personal meanings for themselves (Rosenblatt 1978).

Aesthetic Stance

Rosenblatt (1978, 1991) referred to the "aesthetic" stance and response of reading as reading for deriving pleasure from what we read. This often involves living through the experience of the story and the evoking of feelings and associations. This aesthetic response to literature is crucial to developing an ongoing desire to read. Without the expectation of pleasure, and without the satisfaction of a pleasurable feeling from reading, people would not desire to read.

As teachers, we need to understand each child and see to it that we give all children many and continuous opportunities to anticipate reading their own choices of literature, with pleasure. Likewise, we need to ensure that we provide a classroom atmosphere and climate conducive to the pleasurable enjoyment of their selected literature. We must also always remember that what is pleasurable to one child may not be pleasurable to another child. By knowing and working with our students, we can anticipate some of their needs, desires, and motivations; however, only the individual students themselves can really know what is pleasurable to them.

Efferent Stance

Rosenblatt (1978, 1991) also referred to "efferent" reading. *Efferent* means to carry away information from reading and, ideally, relate it to what the reader already knows. When readers seek out or take information from reading materials, they are responding to the reading in relation to what they previously knew. Diverse learners, and in fact, all learners, may carry away different information from a particular reading. This must be understood and respected by the classroom teacher.

Additionally, Rosenblatt (1985) pointed out that almost every reading experience calls for a balance between aesthetic and efferent stances. As readers read, they move back and forth between aesthetic and efferent stances or purposes (see Figure 1–2). But, she and others (e.g.,

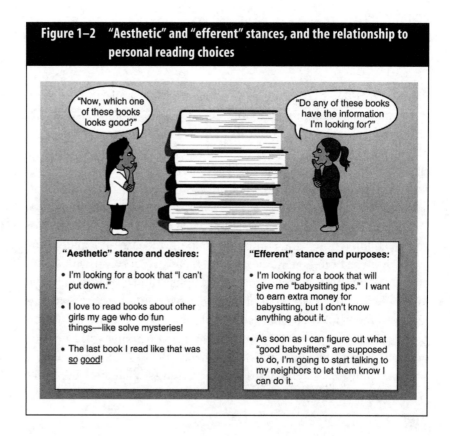

Figure 1–2   "Aesthetic" and "efferent" stances, and the relationship to personal reading choices

"Now, which one of these books looks good?"

"Do any of these books have the information I'm looking for?"

"Aesthetic" stance and desires:

• I'm looking for a book that "I can't put down."

• I love to read books about other girls my age who do fun things—like solve mysteries!

• The last book I read like that was *so* good!

"Efferent" stance and purposes:

• I'm looking for a book that will give me "babysitting tips." I want to earn extra money for babysitting, but I don't know anything about it.

• As soon as I can figure out what "good babysitters" are supposed to do, I'm going to start talking to my neighbors to let them know I can do it.

Many, Wiseman, and Altieri 1996 and others they reviewed and cited) indicate that literature should be read and responded to by readers for primarily aesthetic stances—in other words, for pleasurable reasons. While I agree with this, I also believe that readers can and will read for efferent purposes (i.e., to seek information) and still derive satisfaction from the reading. However, for this to happen, readers must be truly motivated to seek and read the information. Figure 1–2 illustrates this conception of the aesthetic and efferent stances and shows how they can each relate to and enhance personal reading choices.

Reflection Activity 1.2

For what aesthetic purposes or desires do you read? For what efferent purposes might you be interested in reading? What do you do as a teacher to help children develop a desire to read and anticipate it with pleasure?

Personal Feelings and Beliefs

One important area that should not be overlooked is children's personal feelings about themselves as readers, and their beliefs and understandings concerning reading. Because of the research and literature in affective factors (e.g., Alvermann and Guthrie 1993; Cramer and Castle 1994), we know that children who have made positive associations with reading tend to read more often, read for longer periods of time, and read with greater interest. Children's self-perceptions as readers can influence their overall orientations and associations to reading (Henk and Melnick 1995). It is therefore very important that the classroom teacher is aware of each child's attitudes (McKenna and Kear 1990) and feelings about himself or herself as a reader, as well as each child's beliefs and understandings about reading.

Two assessment instruments are recommended for classroom teachers' use. One is a rating scale developed by Henk and Melnick (1995), the Reader Self-Perception Scale, which contains thirty-three questions with which students are asked to indicate their agreement or disagreement using five possible choices. The questions are designed to measure how each student feels about himself or herself as a reader. A second suggested assessment instrument for determining your students' beliefs and understandings about reading is the Reading Interview (Goodman, Watson, and Burke 1987, 219–220). This assessment uses ten open-ended questions to probe students' ideas and concepts.

Classroom teachers could use these or similar assessments (e.g., McKenna and Kear 1990, and others found in various reading assessment texts), or their own probing questions, to discover how their students feel about themselves as readers, and how each of their students views the reading process. Using a combination of ideas from the works of Henk and Melnick (1995) and Goodman, Watson, and Burke (1987), as well as Flippo (2003), I have developed some questions to help get you started. In Figure 1–3, you will find some open-ended questions to uncover children's feelings and beliefs as they relate to reading. In Figure 1–4 the questions include motivations as well as feelings and beliefs. Additionally, you could certainly develop more questions tailored to your own individual students. These inventories can also be found in Appendix C. Feel free to copy and use them as you wish.

Clearly, students' feelings and perceptions about reading will affect the personal choices they make about reading. Classroom teachers will need to consider their understandings regarding these feelings, as well as their understandings regarding the importance of the aesthetic stance of reading and the personalization of meaning each reader gets from a reading, to facilitate development of students' personal reading. This is a tall order, but in the chapters that follow, each of the six aspects of personal reading will be discussed, with these understandings serving as a foundation to the discussions. I want to be clear that I do not see personal reading as a separate or discrete part of the early childhood or elementary school day. Rather, I see development of personal reading as an important goal of the classroom teacher; and the application of personal reading as a weaving into the curriculum of meaningful, interesting, motivating, and self-selected reading materials for all students, with full consideration for their diverse feelings, desires, and needs (see Figure 1–5).

Figure 1–3   Uncovering children's feelings and perceptions about reading

Uncovering Children's Feelings and Perceptions About Reading

1. If you were asked to describe yourself as a reader, what would you say?
   _____
   _____
   _____
   _____
   _____ .

2. What do you think your last year's teacher thought about you as a reader? Why?
   _____
   _____
   _____
   _____
   _____ .

3. How do you feel when you read? Do you feel good? Do you feel bad? Why?
   _____
   _____
   _____
   _____ .

4. What do you think your parents and family think about your reading? Do they think you are a good reader? Do they think you are a bad reader? Who thinks these things? Why?
   _____
   _____
   _____
   _____
   _____ .

5. Who is a good reader that you know? What makes him or her a good reader?
   _____
   _____
   _____
   _____
   _____ .

Figure 1–4   Feelings, beliefs, and motivation inventory

Feelings, Beliefs, and Motivation Inventory

1. I like to read most when I _____
    _____
    _____
    _____ .

2. When I read, I feel _____
    _____
    _____
    _____ .

3. I would read more if _____
    _____
    _____
    _____ .

4. I read better than _____ but not as good as _____ .
    I could be just as good if _____
    _____
    _____
    _____ .

5. Here is a picture of me reading:

    I feel _____
    _____
    _____ .

Figure 1-5 Weaving into the curriculum meaningful, interesting, and self-selected reading materials for all children

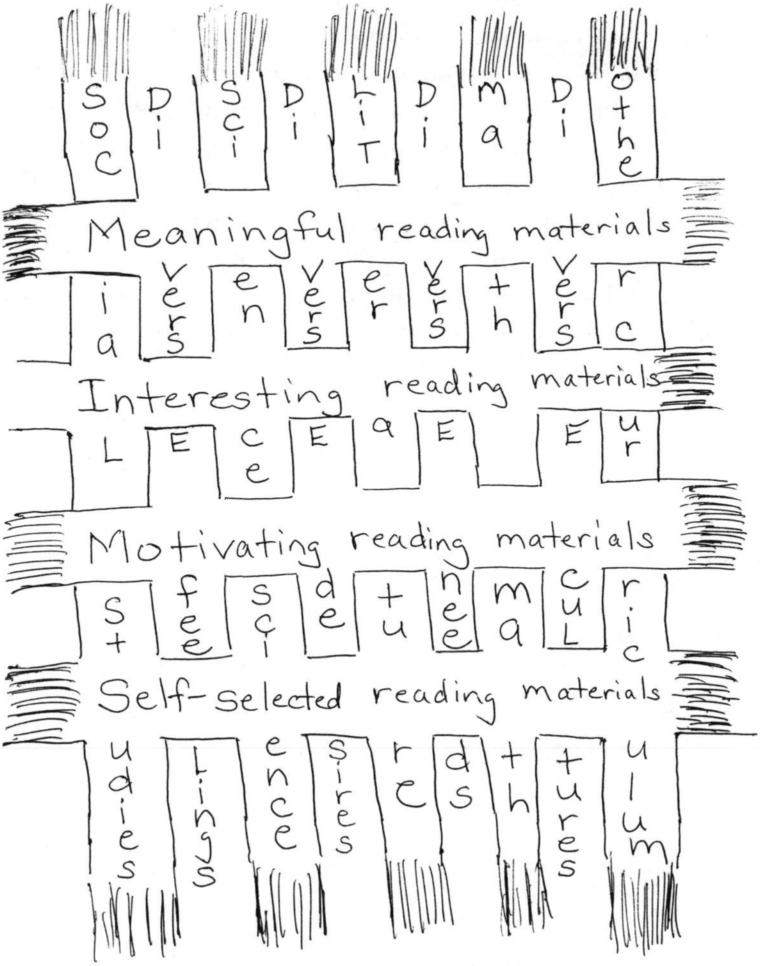

Understanding Personal Reading: A Summary

Personal reading encompasses all the reading that children choose to do. These choices include reading for pleasure, as described by Rosenblatt's (1978, 1991) "aesthetic" stance, as well as reading for "efferent" purposes, which Rosenblatt describes as for seeking information. These choices are always influenced by the readers' feelings about themselves; beliefs about reading; and their culture, community, and family. The classroom teacher must keep all of this in mind as she seeks to develop personal reading opportunities, including those that can take place within the regular classroom curriculum, for all children.

Try It Out

1. Discuss with students what personal reading is, as opposed to the more academic or teacher-directed type of school reading that they are often required to do in the classroom. Ask when they usually do their personal reading outside of school. Ask for ideas of how they can have more time for their personal reading both in and out of school. Create lists of these student-generated ideas with the students and post them in the classroom.

2. Have students discuss reasons why they personally read. As students discuss and share their reasons, develop a list and keep the list posted in the classroom. Encourage students to review and add to this list.

3. Have your students interview each other regarding how they feel about books and reading. In small groups, have students brainstorm good interview questions to ask and then have them share the questions with the whole class. Or if needed, in a large group, generate questions with the students that they can ask each other. Record the questions to be used for the interviews on the chalkboard. Students conduct interviews and take notes on the answers they get to their questions. Then they can present the information about how their classmates view reading and books to the whole class or in a small group.

4. Bring your class to the school library. Give them a quick tour of the library so that they are aware of the many different kinds of books available to them and where such books are located. Tell them that they have a very important task—to find the book that they most want to read. Allow your students to pick any book, without giving them boundaries regarding what kind of book they could choose—just something they find interesting and want to read. Back in the classroom, ask students to share their reasons for making their choices. Give students some classroom time to actually begin reading their books and suggest that if they would like, you can give them time each school day to continue reading their book selections.

Current and New Interests

2

When a teacher can help children find books that match the children's own unique, diverse interests and motivations, the teacher is indeed enhancing personal reading. To facilitate the pursuit of individual students' interests, the teacher first helps students identify what they find interesting. Then the teacher may need to find ways of addressing the diverse interests of some of them, helping other students to deepen their interests or to develop new ones. This can be done in several ways. What follows is a brief discussion of the various possibilities for your consideration.

Interest Inventories and Questions

Numerous interest inventories have been developed and published in literacy education texts. Most of these contain a list of questions to ask children about their reading interests, sports interests, television interests, and hobbies. Additionally, there are often questions concerning favorite pets, animals, movies, games, and music. The intent of these interest inventories is to inquire into the students' individual interests and preferences.

Interest inventories typically use open-ended questions, where students write, list, or tell their interests, or check or circle their choices. Most authors have suggested that teachers of young students or students who may need support read the questions to the children individually and assist them by taking dictation and writing responses to the open-ended questions. Teachers of older or more independent students are usually directed to give the questions to the students, who then record their own responses. Although I do not disagree with these methods, I favor the more personal approach of a one-to-one, teacher–student discussion of interests. This will demonstrate to your students that their individual interests are really important to you, and will ensure you that each child's response is accurate rather than a result of misunderstanding the question or directions. I also favor open-ended questions that provide more opportunities for students to express their true interests and thoughts.

I have provided three interest inventories (sets of questions) that you might want to use (see Figures 2–1, 2–2, and 2–3). Or you may prefer to develop your own interest inventory. It is likely that your own interest inventory will be more appropriate for your students because you will be aware of any special community, regional, ethnic, cultural, and sociocultural conditions that would add to the interests and desires of your students. You could also choose to use one of my lists as a base, delete any of my questions, and then add your own special questions and interest areas to anticipate and fit your students' diverse interests and needs. My interest inventories are also included in Appendix C. Feel free to copy them and use them as you wish with your students. You will note that the Figure 2–1 inventory is more appropriate for upper-elementary-grade students. The inventory in Figure 2–2 may work best for the middle-elementary years (grades 3 and 4); however, children of upper or lower elementary grades could reveal much about their reading interests from this inventory as well. For younger students, in kindergarten through grade 2, the Figure 2–3 inventory should work best.

Figure 2–1   The Flippo interest inventory

The Flippo Interest Inventory

Directions: This inventory can be given orally to both younger and older students, or you can have your older students complete it independently. To obtain accurate and complete information, it is recommended that you record students' oral responses exactly as they give them to you. If students ask for assistance with their written responses, feel free to help them.

1. What are the things (topics) you like most to read about? Why?

2. What are the things you like most to do? Why?

3. Are there some new things (topics) that you are interested in learning about? Why?

4. What would you like to do when you grow up? Why? List or tell everything you can think of that you would really like to do.

5. What kinds of things do you like to read about—or watch TV, videos, or movies about—just for fun or excitement? Why?

6. Have you heard or read about anything new or unusual (in school or at home) that you would like to learn more about? Why?

7. Do you like to do things by following directions such as cooking, building or assembling, sewing, or writing away for things? Which do you like? Why?

8. What is your favorite kind of music?

9. Do you have any special hobbies? What are they? Why are they especially interesting?

10. Do you have any favorite sports? What are they?

(Continues)

Meeting Individual Interests

Once you have assessed your students' interests, the real challenge begins. Now you must ask and answer the question, How can I meet these varied interests and diverse needs? The answer is (1) to provide

Figure 2–1 (Continued)

11. Do you have any pets? What kinds?

12. Are you interested in any role-playing games? If so, which ones? (Note: You may want to reword these questions for use with younger students.)

13. Do you have some special concerns or problems that you would like to explore, work on, or change? If so, would you like some help finding resources or information? (Indicate to students that they do not have to answer these questions, but if they do, their answers will be confidential. Also note that you will need to reword these questions for use with younger students.)

14. If you could do anything in the world and money was no object, what would you like to do? Why?

15. If you could go anywhere in the world and money and time were not problems, where would you like to go? Why?

16. What are the names (titles) of your favorite books? Who are your favorite authors?

17. Of all the books and authors listed in item 16, which/who is absolutely your favorite book and favorite author? Why?

18. If you wanted to tell people about this book (and/or author), and convince them to read it (or read other books by the author), what would you say?

19. If some people wanted to give you a number of books, magazines, or other types of printed materials to read, what kind should they give you? Why? Can you name some particular titles?

20. If a writer told you she would write a book, just for you, about anything, but she needed to know what you would want in the book, what would you say?

many opportunities for students to go to and use the library, (2) to provide many opportunities for students to peruse and have time to read the various reading materials (e.g., genres of books, magazines) you bring into the classroom for them, and (3) to find other resources for special problem and need areas. You may also need to guide the more reluctant readers toward their indicated interests and gently suggest that they self-select and explore those materials. However, because

Figure 2–2 The "best books" inventory

The "Best Books" Inventory

1. The names of the books I like best are _____
   _____
   _____
   _____
   _____
   _____
   _____
   _____
   _____ .

2. They are about _____
   _____
   _____
   _____
   _____
   _____
   _____
   _____
   _____ .

3. They are really good because _____
   _____
   _____
   _____
   _____
   _____
   _____
   _____ .

4. I would like to read more books about_____
   _____
   _____
   _____
   _____
   _____
   _____
   _____
   _____ .

self-selection and self-motivation are very important to personal read-ing, take care to only suggest and offer choices and options. Remember the aesthetic stance! You want children to read because they desire to.

A wide variety of literature is available on almost any topic or inter-est area, and for many problem areas, too. Your school or public librar-ian can help you find the most current indexes of children's literature, which contain lists and abstracts of books and other reading materials

Figure 2–3   My "favorites" inventory

My "Favorites" Inventory

Directions: The teacher of early-grade children would read the following statement to the children.

Statement: "Lots of people are happiest when they're doing their favorite things. Please draw a picture of yourself doing your favorite things. Let's call it 'favorite things'. "

When each child is finished with his picture, the teacher circulates around the classroom and asks each child to tell what favorite things are in the picture. Using sentence strips, the teacher writes the favorite things and attaches the listing to each child's picture. Children are encouraged to hang their pictures with the listings up for display and tell the other youngsters about their favorite things.

classified by genre, topic, subject, and author. Additionally, many excellent professional books are available that suggest literature by topic and interest area, genre or type of literature, age level, and ethnicity. For example, see Galda and Cullinan (2006) for extensive discussions of and suggestions of children's literature; see Trelease (2001) for suggested read-alouds; see Stoll (1997) for a wide variety of magazines classified by age/grade and subject; and see Harris (1997) for children's literature suggestions for a variety of multiethnic literature. Also, Rudman (1995) provides literature suggestions to help deal with special problems, situations, and issues (i.e., divorce, death, abuse, aging, gender roles, and heritage). Appendix A and B, at the back of this book, contain a more complete list of sources.

Remember, children's interests and needs are not standard in any way. Do not limit your students to only the area you define as recreational reading or deter them from reading in areas of their interests or needs. As shown, for example, in Figure 2–1, children may genuinely have an interest in academic areas and more practical areas in addition to fiction or more recreational types of reading. Meeting the individual current interests of all your students must include all areas, purposes, and types of literature.

Pursuit of Students' New and Developing Interests

The use of an interest inventory, with questions you design or add for your particular students, will be a good indicator of their new and developing interests and needs. Additionally, your own observations while teaching your students will be another important guide to emerging interests and possible problems or projects they might want to pursue through reading.

Children, however, may need guidance with their new and developing interests. Often they are not familiar enough with a topic or interest area to know how or where to find appropriate literature. Your role should be that of a facilitator, offering suggestions, possible choices, and other options to help match books to children's diverse interests and motivations. You will need to use some of the available and most current professional books, as suggested, as well as indexes in the school, public libraries, or online, and other sources to locate appropriate reading materials.

Some of your students will benefit the most from the individual help of a librarian, who could suggest available and interesting books and other literature relevant to their particular developing interests and needs. The school librarian is one of the classroom teacher's best resources and should be consulted for professional help whenever possible.

Additionally, you could ask students probing questions to help them verbalize their desires and needs regarding their search for particular literature on particular topics. For example, you could ask:

1. Do you wish you could get some help finding a book you really like?

2. What kind of help do you think you need?

3. Who would you like to help you?

4. When would you like this help?

5. Is there more assistance or more information you need, and where and how do you think you could get this assistance?

Promoting Students' New and Developing Interests

When you have observed or noted an emerging or developing interest in a student, you will need to nurture it carefully. The student may not even realize he is really interested yet. Additionally, a more reluctant reader may balk at the idea that she is really interested in reading anything at all!

How do you hone and nurture these emerging or developing interests? In a low-key way—by making subtle suggestions and by making assignments conducive to the pursuit of those developing interests. Here classroom teachers can really show their know-how and professionalism: You can design assignments related to the school's curriculum (e.g., reading, writing, researching) and your content subjects (e.g., science, social studies) that will enhance those developing interests. (For instance, Mrs. Argueta, a fourth-grade teacher, designed her rainforest assignment to allow students to read and research areas related to their personal interests. One girl, Carmen, used this as an opportunity to read and gather information about snakes and reptiles—which she was very interested in [Flippo 2004].) When students are truly interested in something, they will usually read about it, as long as you approach them with sensitivity to their feelings, needs, and desires. Remember that self-motivation and self-selection are the overall indicators of personal reading and that the real purpose of reading instruction is the development of individuals who will engage in personal reading for pursuit of their interests, needs, recreation, practical and academic purposes, and for just pure pleasure.

Some reflection questions that classroom teachers can ask themselves, to review the curriculum and other potential opportunities to promote students' new and developing interests, include:

1. Are there curriculum areas we will be working on that provide opportunities to explore some specific interests of my students?

2. Are there ways of "working in" some of the other interests?

3. Can I create reading and writing assignments that are open-ended enough to accommodate students' specific interests?

4. What other arrangements can I make to be sure that my students really have opportunities to read in their desired interests?

5. What other resources do I need to help me accommodate every student's reading desires and needs?

6. How can I include the student's family in these efforts?

Reflection Activity 2.1

Can you think of other questions that a classroom teacher should consider or review to help make sure he or she is doing everything possible to facilitate students' pursuit of their reading interests and needs?

Introducing New Literary Genres

Students can benefit from the opportunity to "discover" literature that is new to them. Sometimes this new literature becomes a favorite. It also broadens the experience of students who have had little previous literary exposure. In *Assessing Readers* (Flippo 2003) I describe the literary immersion ideas of Brown and Cambourne (1990). What follows is a brief summary of this process designed to help students discover various genres of literature, one at a time, by being immersed in the literature for a period of time. Literary immersion can be successfully done with children from early childhood through elementary classrooms, as well as with older students (in middle, high, and postsecondary school).

The teacher selects a narrative genre to begin with, in which he immerses the entire classroom for several weeks. For instance, Brown and Cambourne (1990) begin with fables, fairy tales, and myths. The classroom is stocked with a huge collection of this literature, and the children and teacher read nothing but fables for three or four days. Once children have had this experience with fables, the teacher has a whole-class meeting, and the children discuss fables. ("What makes a fable a fable?" etc.) Then, using large chart paper, the teacher solicits generated knowledge or criteria for a fable. The children are encouraged to compare their generated knowledge with a recognized authoritative source, such as an encyclopedia. Children are encouraged to write their own fables. Then, for another four days, children are immersed in fairy tales. The same procedure is used to generate their learned knowledge of fairy tales. Finally, to conclude this genre, children spend an equal amount of time reading, generating knowledge about, and then writing myths.

Throughout the school year, the classroom teacher continues to immerse children in various literature for approximately three-week periods, moving from narrative to expository text. Charts with criteria for all the literature sampled and studied are maintained and displayed in the classroom (extrapolated from Flippo 2003, 246–47).

Ideas for the wide varieties of literature that your students may enjoy can be found in most children's literature books. You may want to consult one or more of these many professional resources for locating children's literature suggested in Appendix A. In addition to those, Buss and Karnowski (2000) and Rickards and Hawes (2005) are helpful.

Current and New Interests: A Summary

Using interest inventories or selected questions, classroom teachers are encouraged to learn about their students' existing as well as developing interests and motivations. Once teachers know of these interests and desires, they can do everything possible to hone and nurture them. Teachers can suggest literature to match students' interests, giving many choices and options. Teachers can also develop academic assignments that will give children a chance to weave their interests into the assignments, exploring their current and new or developing interests further (see Figure 1–5). Teachers can also introduce new types of literature to help students discover new genres that satisfy their interests, motivations, needs, and tastes. Personal reading and study do not have to be separated from school and study work. Instead, they can enhance them.

Try It Out

1. Social interactions with peers can stimulate various interests in children. Book discussions in which students share their favorite books with each other can be very motivating in piquing students' interests in new topics or areas.

2. Set aside time in your schedule for a trip to the public library, if it is within walking distance of your school. If not, enlist the help of parents. The public library is a great place for students to discover new interests and spark motivations. Arrange for children to begin applications for their own library cards. These applications should be taken home to their parents/families for signatures and approval. Talk about the wonderful books they can check out and later take home to read. Facilitate the application process by later collecting the parent-approved application forms and returning them to the library, where you can pick up the children's new library cards. (Or plan and anticipate a second field trip to the library for this purpose. The students will look forward to and savor the next trip.) Collaborate with the librarian to enhance the learning experience. (For example, in advance of your visit, have books set aside for your students in the various areas or things they are most interested in; have new and exciting, popular books on display; arrange for the librarian to read aloud one or more books to the children.)

3. There are many search engine websites available on the Internet, such as Google and Yahoo. Have students use one of these sites to look up children's books related to a topic in which they are interested. A simple search, such as for "children's books about puppies," would likely produce large results and show a student the wide variety of resources available on his or her topic of interest.

    As an extension, have the students cross-check their Internet research list with books available in the school's library or at the public library. Children can print the titles of all the books on their topic of interest that are available in the library, so they can locate them during future library visits.

Reading for Recreational Purposes

Recreational reading is a very important aspect of personal reading. As a teacher, one of your most important roles is to encourage and model recreational reading inside and outside your classroom. You will want your students to be aware that reading can be pursued as a recreational activity that refreshes, relaxes, and restores; and certainly, it can be a very enjoyable pursuit.

One way to build recreational reading into your classroom schedule is to provide some specific time for it each day. During this time, all members of the classroom, including you, the teacher, will set aside their other work and activities to read their books or materials of choice—just for recreational purposes. Other ways to promote recreational reading include: allowing for ample unscheduled or unstructured free-reading time in the classroom every day; encouraging and modeling that children (and you) read books at home for recreational purposes—just to relax and enjoy; and reading enjoyable good books and other "good taste" literature to your students each day.

Sustained Silent Reading (SSR)

The specific, structured quiet time set aside for recreational reading, as just described, is often referred to as Sustained Silent Reading (SSR). It was introduced in 1968 by Fader and McNeil in their book *Hooked on Books: Programs and Proof.* Fader and McNeil called it USSR, the *U* standing for *uninterrupted,* to emphasize the idea that for a particular time period, everyone reads, and no interruptions of any kind are permitted. Many reading educators still encourage the use and ideas of SSR today, even though some use other names like "Drop Everything and Read" (DEAR) time. Whatever you call it, the objectives seem to be the same; that is, to (1) provide students with a specific quiet time for their silent reading, (2) allow students to observe models of appropriate silent reading behavior, (3) provide opportunities for students to sustain their silent reading for longer and longer periods of time, (4) convey to students that reading is important, (5) indicate to students that everyone can read, and (6) develop a sense of trust between the teacher and students that students are individually pursuing reading.

SSR is appropriate for most students of all age groups. It can be implemented in early through the upper-elementary grades by classroom teachers or in a middle or secondary school setting. There have been SSR programs implemented in entire schools, where all students, teachers, administrators, and other school staff (custodial, cafeteria, office) participate. The key benefit of schoolwide SSR programs is the modeling of reading and the accompanying message that reading is important and everyone can do it.

How can you implement SSR in your classroom? It is important to set aside a specific time for recreational reading each day, to encourage students to keep their recreational reading available at their desks, and to keep your recreational reading available and visible on your desk. You should also do the following: (1) Have in your classroom many additional materials that are interesting and enjoyable so that students who forget or finish their books can select from these; (2) have a timer or alarm clock available to time the SSR experiences; and (3) select an appropriate length of time for SSR based on the age and maturity of your students. Typically, with younger students, you may want to begin with only five minutes, and for older students you could begin with ten minutes. Once the routine is established, the time can be gradually increased. There are no specific time regulations, but it might be realistic to eventually have the SSR last ten to fifteen minutes in the early childhood grades, and twenty to thirty minutes for the upper-elementary grades. The use of an alarm clock or timer will allow you and your students to relax and read without watching the clock.

Finally, classroom teachers can do a number of things to enhance the SSR experiences for their students. These include but are not limited to (1) developing a classroom library with diverse and interesting books and other printed materials for teacher and student SSR selection (Allington 1994); (2) encouraging less-abled students to read series books with predictable characters, settings, and plots (McGill-Franzen 1993); (3) permitting students with special needs to use audio "talking books" and digital "e-books," including technology such as Sony's Mobipocket or Palm E-Book Reader, during SSR sessions; and (4) scheduling cooperative-learning activities after SSR sessions to promote authentic and integrated listening, speaking, reading, and writing experiences (Leal 1993; Morrow and Sharkey 1993). Working with parents and other family members to strengthen the home-literacy environment and to establish an SSR program with families would also be advantageous (France and Hager 1993). Overall, reports Krashen (2004), in-school *free-reading* studies show that the more free voluntary reading (FVR) students do, the better are the results in their reading comprehension, writing style, vocabulary, spelling, and grammatical development. Free voluntary reading can be encouraged at home, as well as in the classroom, and the results have proven to be very advantageous to children's literacy development in many areas; plus they love to read!

Unstructured Free-Reading Time

Unstructured free-reading time is another option for the classroom teacher. Unlike SSR, unstructured free-reading has no specific time of day and no specific duration of time. In addition, unstructured recreational reading can be done individually; that is, not all the children in your classroom need to participate at the same time.

The unstructured approach offers flexibility to the teacher and children alike. You can offer students the option of unstructured reading time after the early completion of assignments or during other free time. Some teachers may find that it is more appropriate to set up designated times for free-reading options. Or students can choose their own times for recreational reading.

The structured (SSR) and unstructured approaches to recreational reading can, of course, be used concurrently. Or you may choose to use one and not the other. Based on discussions with several classroom teachers, advantages and disadvantages of each approach are listed. Some of these pros and cons include the following:

Structured

Advantages:

1. The students know that a particular time will be reserved every day for SSR.

2. All of the students will be doing the same thing at the same time.

Disadvantages:

1. Some of the students may not wish to participate in reading everyday at the same time.

2. If the entire school participates in the SSR, the time chosen for schoolwide participation may not be convenient for the individual schedule of a given teacher.

Unstructured

Advantages:

1. The reading time is flexible and can take place at the teacher's or student's convenience.

2. The atmosphere is more relaxed, without the occasional anxiety that builds up as the SSR time approaches.

Disadvantages:

1. Supervision of the students who are reading is much more difficult, since the teacher will probably be working with other students on other tasks.

2. The lack of structure or routine may not be in the best interest of inexperienced readers, and they may be less inclined to participate.

Reflection Activity 3.1

What are your experiences with structured reading (such as SSR or DEAR time) and unstructured reading with students? This reading has also been called "free voluntary reading" (FVR) in the research literature. Do you have implementation ideas you might suggest to make free voluntary reading a frequent opportunity in the classroom and at home?

Max, age 5, enjoying free voluntary reading time.

Elena, age 3¹/₂, relaxing with a book and enjoying voluntary reading at home.

Jennifer, age 12, enjoying voluntary reading at home.

Zoe, age 2, absorbed in voluntary reading of books in her bed (before going to sleep).

Reading to Your Students

Sharing literature of all kinds with your students is a wonderful way to encourage recreational reading and help students realize that reading is a refreshing, relaxing pursuit. When you read aloud to your students, you not only are sharing literature with them, you also are "demonstrating reading." In addition, you are creating a pleasant, memorable experience for your students. These experiences can be particularly important for diverse learners and for students who have expressed negative or unhappy feelings and attitudes about reading.

Anderson and colleagues (1985) indicate in *Becoming a Nation of Readers: The Report of the Commission on Reading* that the single most important thing teachers can do for students to help ensure their future success in reading is to read aloud to them. Many teachers also indicate that reading selected books aloud to their classes is their most enjoyable activity associated with teaching. Others extol that the benefits and gains to be made by reading aloud to children are immeasurable (Daisey 1993; Trelease 2001), some researchers have suggested that reading aloud to children also promotes cognitive and emotional challenges without frustrations (Gersten and Jiménez 1994); literacy development (Galda and West 1992; Scott 1994); whole-class unity (Swindal 1993); individual and cultural identity (Gillespie et al. 1994); and appropriate gender, ethnic, and other perceptions (Fox 1993). However, for maximum reading-aloud benefits to occur, some have also suggested (e.g., Hoffman, Roser, and Battle 1993) that teachers have a logical and planned read-aloud program so that children know it is important and that it actually happens in the classroom. What follows is a brief listing of questions and answers you could consider when including reading aloud to children as part of your classroom experiences. These ideas were developed by reviewing various language arts and teaching-with-literature books (e.g., Barton 2001; Hennings 2002; and Tompkins and McGee 1993).

Reading-Aloud Questions and Answers

1. What kind of reading-aloud experiences do I want for my students? What are my options?

   Answer: Many options exist. Some teachers prefer doing all the reading aloud themselves. Other teachers invite fluent readers to read aloud to students, such as other students in the class, the school librarian, older students, parents, or other community members. There are no limits to who can read aloud. The important criteria is that the readers are fluent and present an enjoyable experience for your students.

2. Is Readers' Theater an option? What would it involve?

   Answer: Yes, Readers' Theater is a viable option. Using Readers' Theater, a group of students in your classroom, or from an upper-grade classroom, present their story or script by reading it like a play to other students. Once again, when using Readers' Theater as a read-aloud option, be sure the readers are all fluent and well rehearsed so that the audience has a pleasurable listening experience.

3. Should I consider reading aloud to my students as a "treat" or an "extra" that I can do when we have time, or when they've been particularly good?

Answer: No, reading aloud to your students should not be restricted for use as a reward for good behavior, nor should it be viewed as an extra that can be squeezed in when there is time. Reading aloud should be considered a valuable way of sharing literature with your students and should be done *at least* once each day, more if possible.

4. I teach an upper-elementary grade. Should I be reading aloud to my students?

   Answer: Yes, reading aloud has no age barriers. It can be used with students at all age and grade levels, from the youngest preschool child through students in the middle and even high school years.

5. I think that reading aloud to students is a good idea, but we have so many curriculum requirements in my school, how can I justify the time it will take out of my class schedule each day? What do I tell the principal when she asks?

   Answer: You could say, "Reading aloud to the students introduces them to a wide variety of literature, nurtures their love of literature, models for them what good readers do, introduces them to a variety of authors and genres, gives me a chance to share books with children that they may not be able to read themselves, and gives me an opportunity to turn them on to reading."

Reflection Activity 3.2

How would you explain the importance of the teacher reading aloud in the classroom to a parent who is concerned that it will take precious time away from teaching the *really important* information that the students must know to pass the state's curriculum frameworks' test?

The following list suggests some tips for reading aloud to your students. These tips may help enhance read-aloud performance, but if you are not comfortable with one or more of them, don't feel compelled to include them. The idea is that a certain amount of showmanship, or show-womanship, is sometimes entertaining and enjoyable to your audience. Additionally, you do need to consider where you and the children sit during read-alouds; all children must be able to easily hear you read as well as see any illustrations you display. Obviously, if students can hear, see, and enjoy the read-aloud, they will have more opportunity to get maximum benefits from the experience.

Read-Aloud Tips

1. *Be expressive.* No one likes to listen to an unenthusiastic reader. Expression should not be confined to the voice, since the face can also be used to exhibit an appropriate appearance for the action of the story.

2. *Vary the loudness of the voice.* This should be tailored to fit the action of the story. For tense moments of anticipation, when everyone expects a sudden dramatic event, you can switch to a very soft voice, with slow and deliberate phrases. When the dramatic event does occur, your voice would become much louder.

3. *Show physical movement.* During the course of the reading, you can move around the room, as long as everyone can still hear you and see the illustrations. Physical movement could also entail physical expression with head, arms, and maybe even legs.

4. *Allow discussion during the reading.* Frequently students will become particularly excited about something that has taken place in the story. When this occurs, spontaneous comments and discussions can be expected. This does not indicate impolite behavior on the part of the students but, rather, shows that they are involved in the plot. Stop for a few seconds to let the students share their ideas.

5. *Select appropriate stopping points.* This is an important maneuver in reading aloud. There are specific hints for the selection of good stopping points within most stories, and as you develop your techniques you will be able to identify these points if you preread any stories or books you plan to read to students. Typically, the best stopping points occur when the story reaches its apex of suspense, where everyone who is listening is convinced that the next sentence will answer the question, What's going to happen?

Finally, postreading discussions, rereading of favorite parts of the story, and extension activities often heighten children's enjoyment and awareness of the literature that has been read. Lively postreading discussions could focus on getting students to make connections between the literature read and their personal experiences. These connections promote appreciation and critical thinking. Rereading memorable or favorite parts of the story will provide students with a deeper understanding of the author's intent and the story line. This understanding in turn increases the quality and quantity of students' responses to the literature. Postreading extensions should encourage reflection and rethinking. Independent or cooperative-learning extensions you could use to promote students' insights and personal reactions are creative writing activities, literature journals, art and drama projects, and Readers' Theater, using the story just read as the script (Hancock 1993; Young and Vardell 1993). Another postreading activity could be to have your students critique the story read and recommend literature for future readings (Saccardi 1993/1994) or to add to the classroom library selection (Prill 1994/1995). The selection of related literature (e.g., writing by the same author or within a thematic unit) permits students to explore interrelationships, to discover patterns, and to think more deeply (Hoffman, Roser, and Battle 1993).

Although the next chapter discusses selection of reading materials, and at the end of this book I provide a list of resources, I do want to point out one particular book, which is a favorite of mine and is especially devoted to reading aloud: *The Read-Aloud Handbook* by Jim Trelease (2001). This book contains many helpful suggestions for both teachers and parents. Additionally, it includes an annotated list of many children's books very suited to reading aloud. You could obtain the Trelease book from your library and use it as an additional source for read-aloud literature for your students.

Reading for Recreational Purposes: A Summary

Recreational reading is an important part of the classroom day. This chapter depicts the advantages and disadvantages of structured and unstructured silent reading. Reading aloud to students of all ages each and every day is something that teachers should schedule into the daily classroom curriculum. This provides children with an opportunity to enjoy a variety of literature, listen to a fluent reader read, and observe what good readers do.

Try It Out

1. Allow yourself to share with your students an interesting book that you are currently reading for recreation. Model enthusiasm and share with them what you are enjoying, or (if it applies) what you might not like about the book. This will model literacy sharing with them and also help them express their own thoughts about books they read.

2. We want children to recognize that reading can be fun and enjoyable. An important aspect that contributes to a positive feeling toward reading is a comfortable environment. Set aside a corner, or several corners or sections of your classroom, where students can get comfortable with their books. These areas might contain pillows, blankets, stuffed animal "reading buddies" for younger children, or other objects that would contribute to children's comfort and relaxation as they enjoy their books. Being comfy is important to reading enjoyment. Bring in crates of library books that are divided into many of the interest areas that children have indicated. Be sure to replace the books with new selections of interest as often as possible, so the selection and choices stay fresh and exciting. Children can use these areas for their SSR and DEAR time reading, as well as other reading opportunity times they find throughout the school day.

3. Reading aloud is always a good way to get students interested in new books, but reading the summary on the inside or back cover of some books to students can really strike interest in a book that students might otherwise have passed over as a choice for personal reading. Take time to read several of these summaries or introductions with students. Many books for younger children do not have these book summaries because they are often so short, but the teacher can read the first page or two, or do a picture walk through the book with the students. These are surefire ways to get students interested in reading these new selections. The books

should then be placed in the classroom where students have easy access to them.

4. Students often look up to "celebrities" in their school or community, such as the principal, mayor, firefighters, or police officers. Invite one or more of these individuals into your class to read aloud selected books to the children.

Selection of Reading Materials

Selection of reading materials is probably the most controversial chapter in this book, and one of the most controversial in the field. In fact, this book's main theme is that in order to develop children into readers who really want to read, *children should be matched to books,* considering their interests and motivations for reading. This in turn will develop them into readers who get personal satisfaction from their reading.

The opposite and more prevalent idea, has been that of *matching books to children.* This is usually done by leveling books from easiest to hardest, and then attempting to match the leveled books to the children. This, it is believed by many, will develop them into readers because the books are just "at the right level" for them to read. "Reading levels" are the prime means of this matching, rather than children's interests and motivations. Take a look at Figures 4–1 and 4–2, which illustrate these divergent ideas concerning book selection for children.

Even though I firmly believe in the importance of continuous assessment of children's reading strengths, strategies, and needs for appropriate decisions regarding reading instruction (e.g., Flippo 2003), I also firmly believe that students who are really interested and motivated to

Figure 4–1 A view of book selection: Matching children to books

read something, will in fact choose it and read it: for example, the lack-luster or seemingly poor reader who *will* read and understand the driver's licensure handbook, even though he has not been willing to read and answer questions for any of the leveled books his teachers have assigned to him. As this scenario indicates, the powers of interest and motivation should not be underestimated or overlooked.

Other writers support the importance of students' self-selection of their books and other reading materials rather than the assignment of books or decisions about what is appropriate for children to read (Murrill 2005). Murrill provides examples of these reader-response

Figure 4–2   A view of book selection: Matching books to children

studies from the research literature; they demonstrate that all readers, including children, bring to every book a very complex set of prior knowledge, schemata, assumptions, and memories rooted within each person's individual "self." Connecting with books is more than a simple matter of the child's decoding skills, the level of the book, and so on—because readers connect with their emotions. It does not, therefore, make sense to generalize about books that are "just right" for younger or older children at certain levels, or books that all children should be exposed to (Crago 1993). Hunt (1991) indicated that "the literature *of* the child may not be the same as the literature *for* the child . . . mismatchings are inevitable" (58). Murrill (2005) further explains that the readers themselves are the only ones who can determine what they want to read.

Leveled Books

There are certainly advantages for the teacher in using leveled books and matching those books to the children for instructional purposes. These advantages include:

1. The ease of putting children into instructional groups based on the level of books they have been assigned to.

2. Targeting the instruction to match the level of the books.

3. Saving teachers' valuable time. (It is time-consuming to help match each child's interests, motivations, desires, needs, strengths, and so on, to special books "just right" for each child. When books have already been leveled and are matched to children's levels, much of the teacher's time can be saved for "real" instruction.)

There are problems, too, for the teacher as well as the students, with the use of leveled books:

1. For one thing, teachers do not always know or fully understand how various books have been leveled. The criteria used to level the books are of prime importance. However, because the books come from a reputable publisher or source, some teachers tend to assume that the leveled books will fit their needs, their students' needs, and the context of instruction they believe in.

2. Another problem of using leveled books is that there is much more focus on the books themselves and the leveling process than on the students' real needs, strengths, interests, and motivations.

3. The idea of "matching books to a group of children" is not as individualized and is less likely to be as effective as matching children to books—special books that children select just for themselves (sometimes with the teacher's help in locating these).

Reflection Activity 4.1

What is your experience with "leveled books"? Can you suggest any other advantages of or problems with using them that I have overlooked?

Matching Children to Books

Children can be matched to books and other reading materials in many ways, depending on the teacher's purpose. Selection criteria will have a different focus for different purposes. For example, if the *teacher's purpose* is to select appropriate reading materials for children's reading instruction, then the children's particular skills, strategies, and schemata or prior knowledge will be the prime focus, without forgetting the children's interests and motivations. If a book is being selected for the teacher's *other academic instructional purposes,* such as science or social studies' learnings, then the criteria for selection would include such things as the children's schemata or prior knowledge of the concepts and topics covered in various book possibilities; the difficulty of the concepts and topics for the children who would use the books; and the likelihood that various topics, text features, and organization of the material in the possible books would be interesting or motivating for the children. (See Figure 4–3 for a list of features of text you might want to consider for a particular child; also, Flippo 2003, 223–24; Fountas and Pinnell 1999, 18–19; Opitz and Ford 2001; Rasinski and Padak 2001; and Routman 2000.)

Since the goal of *this* book, however, is to develop children's personal reading, and since personal reading should always involve the self-selection of materials to be read and the self-motivation to read those materials, the criteria for selection and the actual selection of the

Figure 4–3   Features of instructional text and criteria for particular children

Questions to Consider

1. What concepts and topics are covered by the text or book being considered?

2. What about the difficulty of these concepts and topics?

3. Are the various topics and their presentation in this book ones that this/these child(ren) would find particularly interesting and motivating?

4. Do the topics match some of the interests, motivations, and needs of this/these student(s)?

5. What schemata are necessary to understand the concepts and topics of the instructional text or book being considered?

6. What other prior knowledge would be helpful?

7. Would the material in this book *really* add to the learning of the child/children using it?

8. What extensions of the material presented in this text or book would the child/children find interesting and motivating?

books will really be up to each child. That said, the teacher who wants to enhance personal reading development can *help* children with their criteria and selections based on the teacher's knowledge of the child's interests, motivations, and a knowledge of children's literature (including books, magazines, and other available materials) that could be an appropriate match. Teachers can do this by some *gentle* mentions or suggestions, sharing and reading aloud "possible" books, and displaying these books in the classroom.

I also suggest a self-selection "helper" that teachers can post or give children to remind them of the kind of books and motivations they said were of interest or importance. These can be updated by the children as the school year continues. I used 4-inch-by-6-inch lined index cards to create my "helpers." Whenever a card gets lost, crumpled, or has no space left on it, it is easily replaced. If you teach the early primary grades, you will want to use the bigger-size index cards for your students—little ones will need wider lines and more room on their help cards. (See Figure 4–4, try it out as is, or make your own modifications.)

The teacher can additionally provide an easy-to-use method that will help the children "self-monitor" the difficulty of a book for themselves. In Flippo 2003 (224), I describe the five-finger method, which even kindergarten children can use (and older students in elementary school don't seem to mind it, either) to decide if a book is "just right" or comfortable for them.

The Five-Finger Method

- Pick out a book that you would like to read.
- Begin reading the book to yourself.
- When you come to a word you don't know and can't figure out, put one of your fingers on the word.
- Keep reading and continue to put fingers on words you don't know.
- If you use up all your fingers and your thumb, too, on one page, you've come across five words you don't know or can't figure out. Maybe this book is too hard for you right now. If you would like to try the next page, it is okay, or maybe you want to try another book that also looks good to you.

Figure 4–4 Self-selection "helper" for children

Self-Selection   "Helper"   for _____ Date _____

Things I'm very interested in:	Things I want to learn about or how to do:

If children continue to use up all five fingers on many pages of a book, they should be able to self-determine how appropriate it is for them. When I was a classroom teacher, I posted the five-finger method on poster board over the library table and the classroom library shelves as a reminder for the children of how to do it.

Reflection Activity 4.2

Matching children to books is easier said than done, but I have had great results with it. What do you think? What is your experience with it? Do you have any other suggestions to add?

Good Taste Literature

For recreational reading, most reading material should be considered appropriate. Unless your school or school system has a censorship regulation, children should be allowed to read whatever they like, within, of course, the framework of good taste. Good taste does not imply "good literature." Instead, good taste means literature that is acceptable to your school community and to the various sociocultural groups to which you teach. In other words, good taste materials could include comic books; magazines that feature sports, music, cars/hot rods, and movie/TV stars; popular books like series books and novels; and other materials that are considered by the school community and the greater sociocultural community to be acceptable and nonoffensive. Galda and Cullinan (2006) suggest that teachers must be sensitive to the standards of the communities in which they teach but at the same time must protect children's rights to read material that stimulates, informs, and delights them.

Furthermore, it is important for educators to be aware that the International Reading Association, National Council of Teachers of English, and American Library Association all condemn attempts at censorship that try to restrict students' access to quality reading materials. These organizations provide anti-censorship information on their various websites:

- International Reading Association (IRA) www.reading.org.

- National Council of Teachers of English (NCTE) www.ncte.org. NCTE also provides a direct link to their Anti-Censorship Center www.ncte.org/about/issues/censorship.

- American Library Association (ALA) www.ala.org. ALA provides information regarding book challenges, banned books, banned authors, and other issues in their Office for Intellectual Freedom, which can be reached via the ALA website.

You might, finally, want to consult Simmons (1994) on censorship.

As a *respectful* and *respected* teacher in your school community, you will have opportunities to *work with* the parents and families of your students and talk with and educate them about the importance of their children's self-selection of reading materials and books: books that their children identify as good. It would be wrong and unfair to limit their children's choices, and that can happen when censorship prevails. Yet, you must be sensitive to your community and use that sensitivity to make appropriate professional decisions for your own classroom. Remember, the purpose of recreational reading is for refreshment, relaxation, and restoration, not necessarily for reading good literature.

Good Literature

Having made that clear, I do not want to imply in any way that I do not value good literature. On the contrary, good literature is to be valued, appreciated, and savored. Children who have been pursuing their own personal reading selections and tend to select "good taste" literature rather than good literature can still have exposure to "good" literature when the teacher and librarian select good literature to read to them and through self-discovery in the library and classroom. The teacher and librarian should display an assortment of "good" children's literature for children to browse through. When many Newbery and Caldecott Medal books (e.g., see Roginski 1992), other classic children's trade books and stories, and quality materials from various genres are read and shared with children and are readily available for their self-selection, some of them will be selected and read—and reread.

Many lists of this good literature are available to teachers. School and public librarians usually have published lists, anthologies, and indexes of them. Additionally, I have listed in Appendix A and B at the back of this book suggestions for good sources of literature and other resources for your reference and use. But before reviewing these listings, consider the question: What is a good book?

Good Books

Obviously, descriptions of what a good book is will vary greatly and will probably be as diverse as any population who answers this question. Because of this, no one person's answer can really be considered right or wrong for anyone else. Still, the professional literature contains many and varied descriptions of what good books and good literature contain or do, and how to evaluate a book. For example, Hoffman, Roser, and Battle (1993) suggest that good books have enduring stories with meaty plots that promote interest, literacy development, independence, and personal connections. Crawford and colleagues (1994) indicate that good literature will assist students in finding themselves as learners and people, and will help them learn how to negotiate interpersonal relationships. Tompkins and McGee (1993) state: "The best way to evaluate a picture book or a chapter book is to share it with a child and observe his or her reaction and the depth of that response" (63). Finally, Murrill (2005) emphasizes that only the child can decide if a book is good or not. I agree; for me, the most important elements are the child's joy, satisfaction, and involvement with the reading material. If the child loves the book, it is a good one. Once again, remember the importance of the reader's aesthetic stance (Rosenblatt 1978, 1991) discussed earlier in this book.

Elena, age 3¹/₂, fully involved with her "good" book.

The following list of questions may help guide the reading materials you will choose to read and share with your students. This list includes ideas and suggestions I have found in the professional literature, especially in the works of literacy and children's literature professionals (namely, Fox and Short 2003, Harris 1997, and Tompkins and McGee 1993; and also in Galda and Cullinan 2006; Farris 2001; and Hennings 2002). Clearly, if any answer to these questions reveals a problem, then it is strongly suggested that you *not* read the book or story to your students.

Questions to Help Guide Your Selection of Reading Materials for Reading and Sharing

1. Will this book or story hold your students' attention?

2. Does the plot make sense?

3. Are the characters interesting and believable?

4. Do the characters develop as the book or story develops?

5. Are the characters stereotyped, or does the author's presentation seem biased in any way toward or against any particular group?

6. Does the style and language of the book or story seem appropriate to the particular literature?

7. Will your students be comfortable with and understand the style and the language of the material?

8. Does the book or story have a worthwhile overall theme and is it applicable to students' diverse understandings and backgrounds?

9. Does this book appear to be culturally authentic and culturally sensitive?

10. Is this a book or story that all your students will love and ask you to read over and over again?

11. Does this book or story exemplify the most fundamental characteristics of its genre, so that students can correctly generalize it as one example of the genre?

12. When you look at the pictures, illustrations, and images in the book, do they seem to be accurate, authentic, and nonstereotypical representations of women (and girls), men (and boys), people of color, and people of various diverse ethnic and racial groups?

13. If this is a nonfiction book, what are the author's credentials for writing about this topic? Does the content appear to be authentic? If this is a fiction book, did an "insider" or "outsider" perspective inform the book and to what extent does the book succeed in fulfilling its apparent purpose?

14. Is there anything in this book that would embarrass or offend any child in your classroom? Is this a book that you are completely comfortable sharing with a group of mixed-race children, with a group of all-black children, and with a group of all-white children?

Additionally, I came across a webpage from The Council of Interracial Books for Children that provides "10 Quick Ways to Analyze Children's Books for Racism and Sexism" (*www.birchlane.davis.ca.us/library/10quick.htm*). If you want more help with your responses to questions 5, 9, 12, 13, or 14, you might want to consult this site (see also Fox and Short 2003).

A Large Variety of Books Is Good for the Classroom

Do not be dismayed if your students choose to read good taste literature instead of the good literature suggested from the previous questions and the lists in the appendixes. Remember, personal reading involves personal selection and motivation. Be happy and know that you are reaching your intended goals when your students self-select and read for recreation either good taste or good literature. They are reading and learning to use reading as a means of recreation—this is the most important thing! The implication is that you will need to

1. Have a large variety of good taste literature available for the children's perusal and reading, making use of the information you collected from interest questions and other observations.

2. Allow children to bring in their own good taste literature, if they choose to.

3. Have a large variety of good literature available for the children's perusal and reading, according to the information you collected from interest questions and other observations, and from the good literature sources and lists you've found in the professional suggestions near the end of this book. (Some of the good literature might very well fit in with the students' interests.)

4. Have a large variety of good literature available from the good literature lists for children and from librarians' suggestions.

5. Read good literature aloud each day to your students. Children enjoy being read to, and there is much evidence to suggest that reading to children is an important aspect of literacy.

6. Frequently, every week or two, bring in new good taste literature and good literature to the classroom for students' perusal and self-selection, and remove most of the literature that has "been around" for more than two or three weeks. (Feel free to keep "favorite books" for an extended time. Many of your younger or less-developed readers will benefit from repeated readings of their favorite stories and books.)

Selection of Reading Materials: A Summary

This chapter highlights the difference between the practice of "matching books to children" and this book's main theme, "matching children to books," which, together with helping to facilitate their interests and motivations, helps them develop their personal reading. Leveled books are discussed, along with the advantages and disadvantages of using them. Suggestions are presented for matching children to books and self-selection by children of the books they will read.

Included also are discussions of good taste literature (differentiating it from what many consider to be good literature), as well as good books, a guide for the teacher's selection of books to share and read to students, and the need to maintain a varied and large classroom library.

Try It Out

1. Students will likely have opinions about the materials they are reading. It would be useful to attach a recommendation card or paper on the inside cover of each book, magazine, and so forth, in your classroom. After finishing a book, a student could record what he or she liked or enjoyed about the book, or perhaps didn't like. Each subsequent student would be able to read reviews from other students to get more of a sense of the book, and all readers would be welcome to write their own views.

2. If a student really enjoys a book, encourage them to search for it on www.amazon.com and write a reader's review. Also, the New York Public Library has developed an online area for children to read and post their own reviews and ratings for books they have read: On-Lion for Kids Book Reviews http://kids.nypl.org/reviews/books/index.cfm. And of course, students can print out their "published" reviews and display them on a "Students' Publications" bulletin board in your classroom.

3. Have interested students create book jackets. These jackets can include a short synopsis of the book, a description of the main character(s), an intriguing problem, a favorite scene, or how the story related to their everyday life. Encourage artwork on the front or back of the jacket that relates to the story.

4. Have your interested students create written or pictorial summaries and descriptions of their own favorite books and why they like them. This writing activity will provide a meaningful language extension. You can have these available in the reading corner for students who might be looking for a new book.

5. A great place to find books for your classroom is at yard sales. Also, used bookstores and other secondhand stores will oftentimes have great selections on classics as well as other much-loved children's good books, and at a reasonable price.

Reading for Academic Purposes

C hildren's personal reading can include reading for academically oriented purposes if they self-select and are self-motivated to choose these materials. If children display real interest in academic areas (as determined by your observations or in response to your questions), then they may choose to personally read in those interest areas. Using the professional materials, indexes, and anthologies as suggested will help you locate reading materials for these very special academic interest areas. Remember, the goal of personal reading development is to promote individuals who are motivated to self-select reading materials for their own personal purposes and interests. As an elementary teacher, it is important that you give students an opportunity to learn how to find materials that they want to read and then provide opportunities for them to read these materials.

Using Interests to Enhance Content Assignments

The classroom teacher can really capitalize on these academically oriented interests. For instance, if he is teaching a unit on transportation as part of the social studies curriculum in second grade, and he has one student who has a strong current or developing interest in model railroads, the teacher can use that student as a resource or "peer teacher" when discussing railroads. The peer teacher in this case may be able to bring into the classroom model railroad cars from various historical time periods, railroad cars for different purposes, and so on. Additionally, if this student is a real model railroad buff, she may know a great deal about the historical development of the railroad in the United States. If she doesn't already know enough about railroad development, the student might be more than willing to read to learn more about it (if the teacher can assist by providing appropriate sources, or by showing the student how to locate sources) and share and explain to the rest of the class.

Here's another example. Mrs. Argueta, the fourth-grade teacher mentioned in Chapter 2, developed a research assignment that allowed students to explore various aspects of rain forests. Carmen, one of her students, was encouraged to use her current knowledge and interests in snakes and reptiles and extend it to her rain-forest research. Carmen became a peer teacher in Mrs. Argueta's class; by sharing examples of snake skins, photos of reptiles and snakes, and newly found books and websites, she developed her and the class' knowledge of the snakes and reptiles that live in rain forests.

Here's one more example. Obi, an African student in Mr. Friedman's sixth-grade class, is particularly interested in the history as well as the current events of Nigeria. Knowing this, Mr. Friedman encourages Obi to share his knowledge and research with the rest of the class during their study of Africa unit. Because of Obi's interest, he is very happy to read as much as possible about Nigeria and has a wealth of information to share with his peers.

Obviously, many more examples could be given; however, the important message would be the same: Your students are capable human beings who have a broad variety of current and developing interests, and these interests should be tapped and enhanced for students' development. The students can read for their own interests, helping themselves and enjoying their pursuits. Additionally, they can share their learnings with other students, helping these other students as well. This indication of respect for all students' academic abilities and learnings is important if we are to model to children respect and caring for all people (e.g., Tiedt and Tiedt 2005, and many others). It is also important that children are given encouragement and an outlet for displaying their academic interests and related readings.

Reflection Activity 5.1

Can you share other examples from your own experience in classrooms of how students' interests can be used to enhance content assignments? (This is different, of course, from the inverse—or trying to use students' interests to get them to read content material.) Here, the emphasis is on self-selection and self-motivation. Students' special interests and knowledge can be resources for your content instruction.

Assessing Prior Knowledge to Enhance Content Learning

As we have seen, children's prior knowledge and experiences do enhance the learning of various content topics. Although many children have an active interest in topics they know about, or in things they have experienced, some children may not have mentioned these topics during the assessment of their interests. In addition, the prior knowledge and experience of learners in your classroom can help you make decisions *about* instruction, as well as using the students' interests and motivations *for* instruction.

Assessing the Students

To adapt your content instruction (e.g., social studies, sciences, and so on) to your individual students' prior knowledge and experience, you must first assess your students and find out "where they are" or "where they are coming from" in regard to the content you hope to teach. Specifically, you can informally assess them, seeking answers to these questions:

1. What do my students already know about the content or concept under consideration?

2. Do my students have some misconceptions about the content or process, and if so, what are these misconceptions?

3. Do my students have the vocabulary, reading, study, and writing background to handle this content or concept?

4. If not, what specific vocabulary, reading, study, and writing abilities or strategies might be a limitation to my students?

5. To what degree are my students interested in this content or concept? If interest is lacking, is there something that the students are interested in that can be related or used in some way with this particular content or concept?

An informal approach, such as having children write, diagram, or draw what they know about a given content, topic, or concept is an excellent initial assessment procedure. Students' writings, diagrams, or drawings and related discussion can provide you with an idea of the depth of their knowledge, possible misinformation or misconceptions, completeness of information, knowledge of related vocabulary, and interest. A follow-up activity such as a preview or introductory library assignment (for older elementary students) can also provide additional information regarding their reading, study, and writing abilities as related to the content. You can use these writings, diagrams, drawings, discussions, and preview assignments both to assess your students and to introduce new contents or concepts to them. Also, you will have gathered valuable information to use as a basis for making decisions about instructional goals, organizing for instruction, and adapting the learning environment. Later, you could present material and ideas that the students can accommodate into their present writings, diagrams, or drawings, thus building on their prior knowledge. (For more examples, see Flippo 2003, 138–47.) Combined with what you already know about your students' individual interests and motivations, your assessment data will enhance and facilitate the learning of the content you plan for your students to study.

Assessing the Learning Situation

What is the best way to provide instruction and facilitate the learning of a content or concepts? What are the constraints of the learning environment? How much flexibility do you have? Do you have the variety of resources you need? How can you adapt to a lack of resources and the constraints of the learning environment? Instituting assessment procedures to evaluate your learning situation will help you not only to answer these questions but also establish a classroom environment conducive to learning.

We all know that the classroom environment is often not the perfect setting or only place to facilitate all that is to be learned. Each situation, content, or concept presents a new challenge. I am not suggesting that you completely reorganize your classroom for every new concept you teach or present. However, I am suggesting that you be aware of the environment and do your best to develop instructional situations that are conducive to the needs of the students and to the needed resources and learning situations for the contents or concepts you hope to teach.

Deciding Instructional Goals and Content

When you have assessed your students and the learning situation, you are in a better position to make decisions about your instructional goals and content. Figure 5–1 presents an example of a completed checklist developed by Ms. Curtis, a second-grade teacher, as she assessed her students' prior knowledge, experiences, and interests related to the study of transportation. Looking over Figure 5–1, you will see that this teacher first assessed the children's familiarity with a full spectrum of various modes of transportation (see Question 1 and the responses). Ms. Curtis' purpose was to see whether most of the students had "heard" of or had recognition-level knowledge of these different means of transportation. After a brief class discussion using pictures, the teacher determined that most of the students were familiar with most of the transportation modes suggested, with the exception of trolley cars, hovercraft, and air boats. Additionally, although the children had heard of limousines, only a few really knew what they were. Although the children recognized a hot-air balloon, they did not really associate it with any means of transportation.

Next Ms. Curtis assessed the students' knowledge of the various modes of transportation (see Question 2 and the responses in Figure 5–2). The purpose was to see whether the children could discuss or could indicate more than recognition-level knowledge for each of these modes of transportation. Again, through large- and small-group discussion, this teacher learned that her second graders had some knowledge of most of the types of transportation suggested but there were some misconceptions or misinformation concerning several modes of transportation. Specifically, "limousine" was not an understood concept. Brittany and Daniel thought the teacher was talking about flooring, whereas Chris and Matthew thought it was a type of fuel. Only two students, Nicholas and Jenny, seemed to make some

---

Figure 5–1 Prior knowledge, experience, and interests checklist for transportation (Question 1)

1. What types of transportation are most of my students somewhat familiar with (that is, students can identify or can draw a visual image of)?

	Yes	No	?	Comments
Cars & minivans	✓			
Trucks	✓			
Taxis	✓			
Limousines			✓	Most students seem to have "heard" of a limousine, but only a few really seem to know what it is.
Buses	✓			
Trolley cars		✓		Nicholas, Kristen, & Jenny were the only students who indicated recognition and knew the name when they saw the picture of the trolley car.
Passenger trains	✓			
Subways/mass transit trains			✓	Students called it a "train," but most seemed to know that it was a different type of passenger train than that used on a cross-country trip.
Airplanes	✓			
Jets	✓			
Helicopters	✓			
Balloons			✓	Students recognized the hot air balloon, but they didn't seem to associate it with any means of transportation.
Hovercraft		✓		
Ocean liners	✓			
Freight ships	✓			
Sailboats	✓			
Fishing boats	✓			
Motor boats	✓			
Air boats		✓		
Canoes	✓			
Row boats	✓			
Walking	✓			
Rollerblades	✓			
Bicycles	✓			

---

appropriate associations between limousines and chauffeurs. Again, trolley cars were not really known to most of the children, nor were balloons, hovercraft, or air boats. Also, during this more in-depth level of assessment, Ms. Curtis learned that the concept of "mass transit" was not very clear among the children. Although they had recognition-level knowledge of a subway, on further probing the teacher found a lack of depth and understanding.

The next area Ms. Curtis explored was the students' actual experiences with these different types of transportation (see Question 3 and the responses in Figure 5–3). This teacher wanted to know whether any of her second graders had actually seen or used any of these types of transportation. Here is what she learned: most of the students did have actual prior experiences with cars and SUVs, trucks, buses, fishing boats,

Figure 5–2   Prior knowledge, experience, and interests checklist for transportation (Question 2)

2. What types of transportation do most of my students seem to have some knowledge of (that is, students can discuss or otherwise indicate more than recognition level knowledge)?

	Yes	No	?	Comments
Cars & minivans	✓			
Trucks	✓			
Taxis	✓			
Limousines		✓		Brittany & Daniel thought we were talking about flooring. Chris & Matthew thought we were talking about some type of fuel. Only Nicholas & Jenny associated limousine with a chauffeur.
Buses	✓			
Trolley cars		✓		Kristen, Jenny, and Nicholas knew what a trolley car was. The other students either didn't know at all or weren't offering ideas. Daniel indicated that it was "a thing you pull behind your car."
Passenger trains	✓			
Subways/mass transit trains			✓	
Airplanes	✓			
Jets	✓			
Helicopters	✓			
Balloons		✓		
Hovercraft		✓		
Ocean liners	✓			
Freight ships	✓			
Sailboats	✓			
Fishing boats	✓			
Motor boats	✓			
Air boats		✓		Jessica thought an air boat was like the pirate ship in Peter Pan.
Canoes	✓			
Row boats	✓			
Walking	✓			
Rollerblades	✓			
Bicycles	✓			

3. What types of transportation have most of my students had some experience with (that is, students have actually seen or used this type of transportation)?

	Yes	No	?	Comments
Cars & minivans	✓			
Trucks	✓			
Taxis			✓	Kristen, Jenny, & Nicholas are the only students who indicated riding in a taxi.
Limousines			✓	Nicholas & Jenny had ridden in a limousine on their way to the airport.
Buses	✓			
Trolley cars		✓		
Passenger trains			✓	Nicholas, Pedro, Amy, & Sophie have all traveled on a passenger train. Amy & Nicholas have traveled on trains overnight.
Subways/mass transit trains		✓		
Airplanes			✓	Kristen, Jenny, Nicholas, Pedro & Amy have all traveled by air. They were unsure whether it was on a regular airplane or a jet.
Jets			✓	
Helicopters		✓		
Balloons		✓		
Hovercraft		✓		
Ocean liners		✓		
Freight ships		✓		
Sailboats			✓	Nicholas, Jenny, Kristen, & Chantele all indicated that they have been out on a sailboat on the lake.
Fishing boats	✓			
Motor boats	✓			
Air boats		✓		
Canoes	✓			
Row boats	✓			
Walking	✓			
Rollerblades	✓			
Bicycles	✓			

motor boats, canoes, rowboats, walking, rollerblades, and bicycles. They had no concrete prior experiences with trolley cars, subways/mass-transit trains, helicopters, balloons, hovercraft, ocean liners, freight ships, and air boats. There were some means of transportation with which a few children had prior experiences, but most of the children had no experience. These included taxis, limousines, passenger trains, airplanes, jets (note there was a little confusion over airplanes and jets), and sailboats.

Next Ms. Curtis looked into which modes of transportation most interested her students; she judged their interest by their animation during large-group discussion and other indications of interest like continued discussions, questions, and sharing of experiences (see Ques-

4. What types of transportation do most of my students seem most interested in (that is, students appear animated when discussing these or otherwise indicate interest)?

	Yes	No	?	Comments
Cars & minivans	✓			Many of the students were very excited discussing different types of cars & minivans.
Trucks		✓		
Taxis		✓		
Limousines			✓	Several children, particularly Nicholas, Jenny, Katie, Sonia & Carlos, were interested in limousines.
Buses		✓		
Trolley cars	✓			
Passenger trains	✓			
Subways/mass transit trains	✓			
Airplanes	✓			
Jets	✓			
Helicopters	✓			
Balloons	✓			
Hovercraft	✓			
Ocean liners	✓			
Freight ships		✓		
Sailboats			✓	Nicholas, Jenny, Kristen, Chantele & Carlos were interested in sailboats.
Fishing boats		✓		
Motor boats		✓		
Air boats	✓			
Canoes		✓		
Row boats		✓		
Walking		✓		
Rollerblades	✓			
Bicycles	✓			

tion 4 and the recorded responses in Figure 5–4). Ms. Curtis discovered that the group as a whole was more interested in cars and SUVs, trolley cars, passenger trains, subways/mass-transit trains, airplanes, jets, helicopters, balloons, hovercraft, ocean liners, air boats, rollerblades, and bicycles than any of the other modes of transportation. However, Ms. Curtis also learned that a few children were particularly interested in limousines, a few others in sailboats.

Ms. Curtis looked next at her available materials and other resources (for example, books, magazines, videos, DVDs, catalogs, brochures, and guest speakers) to ascertain what resources were available to provide information on the various transportation modes and their related concepts and issues. As she inventoried these resources, she considered whether any special reading, writing, and study-skill needs or problems

5. What materials or resources do I have or can I get on transportation (that is, books, magazines, videos, catalogs, brochures & guest speakers)? And, are there any special reading, writing, and study skill considerations for use of these materials?

	Yes	No	?	Comments
Cars & minivans	✓			books, catalogs
Trucks	✓			books, catalogs
Taxis	✓			books, guest speaker
Limousines	✓			catalogs, books
Buses	✓			books, schedules (may be difficult for students to read)
Trolley cars	✓			encyclopedias, San Francisco brochures (the reading material may be difficult), video
Passenger trains	✓			books, brochures, video, schedule (difficult)
Subways/mass transit trains			✓	only a subway schedule
Airplanes	✓			video, books
Jets			✓	video, books
Helicopters	✓			books
Balloons	✓			books, video
Hovercraft			✓	only travel brochure (difficult reading)
Ocean liners	✓			books, brochures
Freight ships	✓			books
Sailboats	✓			books, video
Fishing boats	✓			books
Motor boats	✓			books
Air boats		✓		
Canoes	✓			books, brochures
Row boats	✓			books, brochures
Walking	✓			magazines
Rollerblades	✓			book, guest speaker, brochure
Bicycles	✓			books, brochures, guest speaker

might arise (see Question 5 in Figure 5–5). Please note that this teacher was not driven by the availability of materials but was first interested in students' prior knowledge, experiences, and interests concerning transportation and other special considerations before selecting materials.

Finally, Ms. Curtis considered the possibilities for providing the children with needed experiences (see Question 6 in Figure 5–6). Note, once again, the teacher is most concerned about her students' needs and desires; rather than just making decisions based on what is available or easiest, this teacher bases decisions on her students' prior knowledge, experiences, and interests.

6. What types of transportation could we try out and/or have some sort of access to for possible field trips?

	Yes	No	?	Comments
Cars & minivans	✓			
Trucks			✓	
Taxis	✓			
Limousines			✓	
Buses	✓			
Trolley cars		✓		
Passenger trains	✓			
Subways/mass transit trains			✓	
Airplanes	✓			
Jets	✓			
Helicopters			✓	
Balloons		✓		
Hovercraft		✓		
Ocean liners		✓		
Freight ships		✓		
Sailboats	✓			
Fishing boats	✓			
Motor boats	✓			
Air boats			✓	
Canoes	✓			
Row boats	✓			
Walking	✓			
Rollerblades	✓			
Bicycles	✓			

Reflection Activity 5.2

Look over the data for Figures 5–1 through 5–6. Can you predict which transportation modes Ms. Curtis will facilitate study of in the classroom? What types of transportation do you predict she will select to facilitate student experiences? Why?

What individual or small-group research and study areas would Ms. Curtis probably suggest within the transportation study unit? Why? Perhaps a few interested students could study one means of transportation and report their research to the rest of the class? Which students would be likely to do this?

Using Personal Reading to Enhance Literature Studies

The more often your students are given an opportunity to read based on their personal selection, motivation, and interests, the greater likelihood that they will be exposed to a variety of literature. This exposure to a variety of literature and this immersion in a literate environment—your classroom—will help them develop an appreciation for a variety of literary devices, authors, ideas, and concepts, as well as a knowledge of many genres.

Your students will also be learning about the benefits of a literate environment by being in a literate environment. As students read a variety of literary materials, they will begin to develop an appreciation for many aspects of good literature, such as good illustrations, good bookbinding, good paper and print qualities, good plots, interesting characters, and memorable stories. Although they may not express it, you may find that your students are drawn back to some of these excellent pieces of literature to reread them, to look at the illustrations once more, or simply to enjoy and savor a good book.

Students will also begin to develop a better sense of their own preferences. If they have not been in a truly literate environment before, they may for the first time have an opportunity to experiment with their tastes. Students who have come from more literate environments will have opportunities to continue to develop and refine their tastes.

An appreciation for authors and their works is certainly a very desirable and likely outcome. For example, students who are interested in horses may find that a certain author has written several books on horses. Once students *discover* that author and read and enjoy one of her books, it is likely that they will want to read other books about horses written by the same author. Once they read all the author's books about horses, it is also likely that students may read another book on a different topic or subject by the same author. Your students will discover authors and develop a sense of appreciation for many of them.

Often, after reading a number of books by the same author, students begin to observe similarities as well as inconsistencies in situations, plots, characters, and writing style. This can lead them to much greater awareness and a more critical personal reading of the material—a most desirable outcome. For example, when my daughter, Tara, was an elementary student, she was an avid Nancy Drew book series reader. But Tara observed that the main character in each of the books, Nancy Drew, seemed to remain a perennial teenager, approximately seventeen or eighteen years old, and that Nancy Drew had solved over sixty mysteries within a relatively very brief span of time. Tara's awareness of the age and time discrepancies, developed as she read more and more books in the series, resulted in her criticism of the Nancy Drew series' author for apparently failing to realize that some readers would be aware of the age and time inconsistencies in these books. Thus, Tara was acquiring the ability to become a critical and discerning reader.

One of your curriculum goals as a classroom teacher will undoubtedly be to expose your students to a wide variety of literature in many different genres. A knowledge of various types (or genres) of literature is an academic endeavor. Although I again remind you to be sensitive to the importance of students' self-selection and self-motivation, you can very naturally use students' personal reading interests to enhance their genre awareness and appreciation. Here is one example: Natasha loves to read fairy tales. She's indicated this in her responses to the interest questions you posed. Why not allow Natasha to read all the fairy tales she wants for an extended period of time? Using Brown and Cambourne's (1990) literary immersion model, Natasha will immerse herself in fairy tales, and after several weeks of this immersion she will know quite a lot about fairy tales. If you ask Natasha then, "What are fairy tales like?" she can generate her own list of their literary characteristics. She might say, for example: "They often start with the words, 'Once upon a time,'" "They often have kings, queens, princesses, princes, witches, or goblins as main characters," or "They often end with the words, 'They lived happily ever after,' " and so on. Using Natasha's natural desire to read fairy tales, you will have given her a unique opportunity to learn a great deal about the genre of fairy tales. You could also give Natasha opportunities to write her own fairy tales following her immersion, if she wishes, based on the list of characteristics she personally generated. When she writes, Natasha will emulate some of the author craft that a writer of fairy tales must use.

Or take another example: Max is very interested in reading as many mystery books as possible. He is enthralled with Sherlock Holmes and many of the other classics. You let him follow his natural desire to read mysteries. After several weeks of this immersion in mystery books, Max can tell you many characteristics of mysteries. He might, for example, say things like: "They are full of suspense," "The author tries to keep the 'who-done-it' part till the end, but the mystery is always solved," or "Very often 'who-done-it' is a complete surprise to the reader." Again, Max has had an opportunity to be immersed in literature he loves, learning a great deal about that literature. When given an opportunity, Max can write his own mystery using many of the characteristics of a mystery that he himself generated as a result of his literary immersion experience. He can also emulate some of the author's craft involved with writing a mystery, especially the suspense, plot, and character development inherent in this type of narrative. (See Brown and Cambourne 1990 and Flippo 2003 for more examples and step-by-step details of how to implement literary immersion with your students.)

As your students read, they cannot help but be exposed to a variety of ideas and concepts. They will often be exposed to different and diverse cultures, lifestyles, and problems. The sharing of their literary experiences with one another, by discussing good and bad books, by discussing various genres, by discussing interesting ideas and problems noted in the books, as well as the use of their readings within the framework of the rest of the curriculum (in content reading and writing) will encourage and lead to a richer vocabulary and richer experiential base for each of them. In conclusion, as Rosenblatt (1978) has explained, giving students opportunities to write and reflect about their readings helps them unravel their thinking, elaborate their ideas, and clarify their responses.

Reading for Academic Purposes: A Summary

This chapter has discussed three of the academic outcomes of the teacher's awareness of children's interests, motivations, and prior knowledge: using students' interests to enhance content assignments, using their prior knowledge to enhance content learning, and using their personal reading to enhance the study of literature.

The many benefits of these outcomes are discussed and illustrated with examples of their applications. Even though there are often times when the teacher's purpose is the academic learning of his students, teachers are cautioned not to lose sight of the importance of students' self-selection of reading materials and motivations (whenever possible).

Academic purpose, planning, and learning do have a place within the development and encouragement of your students' personal reading.

Try It Out

1. Before beginning an academic unit, it is important to understand what knowledge and beliefs students bring to the topic. It is also critical to understand what aspects of the topic students are *really* interested in knowing more about. This will allow you to provide appropriate instruction and materials, and to differentiate the assignments according to students' indicated interests. Ask students to complete a "KWL" chart at the beginning of the unit to find out what students currently "*K*now, and what they really *W*ant to Know." The "*L*earned" listing of the chart can be completed at the end of the unit by each student.

    Students can research and find the new information *they want to learn* in library books, reference material (e.g., from encyclopedias in the library or on the Internet), on various websites, and from interviews or questions directed to informed organizations and sources through email. Try it out before beginning your next unit!

2. When students are able and willing to share their extra knowledge, encourage them to develop fact-sharing information sheets that can be printed or photocopied for the rest of the class. If they are ambitious, encourage them to make a presentation for the class using Microsoft Power Point or using the overhead projector.

3. Have a place on the chalkboard where *at any time* students can write questions they are curious about and want to have answered. Allow students, if they wish, to volunteer to answer the questions by researching them at the library and on the Internet. You may discover some hidden talents of a student, once you learn about his or her interests, motivations, and desires concerning learning. Children may show their passion for music, art, drama, science, and other specialized areas when they have been encouraged to read in areas of special interest.

4. Have students search out websites that relate to a topic being studied in class. The websites can be "bookmarked" and used as an online reference for other students in the class.

5. Try having an "Author of the Month" club where you and your interested students review many different books by one favorite author. Do a biography discussion of the author and display many of the author's books around the room. Do read-alouds from the books during snack or group time. Try it out!

6

Reading for Practical Purposes

Students often want to read something of a practical nature to help solve a problem, or to help do or make something new or different. They are motivated because they do recognize the problem, or they are really interested in learning to do something new. This type of reading is as much a part of personal reading as all the other aspects already depicted. Classroom teachers should include reading for practical purposes, as indicated by students' interests, problems, and motivations, in their personal reading development efforts. Once again, the results of your interest questions, as well as observations you make about children's motivations, problems, and needs, will be very helpful. When a particular motivation or need is *uncovered*, pay close attention, ask questions (but be sensitive to the child's need for privacy or other special concerns), and take careful notes. In private, let the child know that you will be willing to help in any way that you can. Ask the student to let you know how you could help. Additionally, information you learn from talking with the children's parents and families will provide you with more assistance. (Working with parents and families for students' personal reading development is explored in Chapter 8 of this book.)

Motivations and Needs

The classroom can be a big and daunting place for a student with unfulfilled motivations, worries, or very special practical needs. Some children may not reveal these on an interest inventory; however, sensitive teachers are alert to certain signs, like a student's preoccupation with his own thoughts, expressions of sadness, or sharing of information that seems unusual or uncharacteristic for a particular child. When these signs are noticed, this is perhaps a good time to *gently* probe for more information using questions and activities in class that you can design specifically to give children an opportunity to disclose their preoccupations, current motivations, and needs. If it later appears that no serious problems or needs are revealed, the information gleaned from these questions and activities still provide an update of a student's most current motivations; assisting the teacher to display or show children some books that may currently satisfy their motivations and needs.

The questions and activities should meet the age group of your class; however, in Figures 6–1, 6–2, and 6–3, I provide a few examples. All students in the class should be involved so that no one child seems to be singled out. These lists can also be found in Appendix C.

Reflection Activity 6.1

How do you think a teacher should proceed after gleaning sensitive information about students' motivations and special practical problems or needs? Are there specific suggestions, cautions, or experiences that come to mind?

Issues and Problem Solving

Just as adults have issues and problems, children often have them, too. Although some of the problems may seem relatively small from a grown-up perspective, to the children they feel big and significant. Many problems facing youngsters in schools today actually are quite serious.

Figure 6–1   Questions for uncovering motivations and practical needs

Questions for Uncovering Motivations and Practical Needs

1. Is there something special that you would like to learn how do do?

2. Is there something special that you would like to get more information about, or that you have to do?

3. Is there something special that you would like to share with the class?

4. Is there something special that the teacher can help you with?

5. Is there something special that someone else in our class, or in our school, can help you with? Who?

6. When you don't come to school, what kind of things do you like to do?

7. When you don't come to school, what kind of things do you have to do?

8. Who do you do these things with?

9. Who would you like to do these things with?

10. If you could wish for three things, what would you wish for?

However, there are resources available to help, and teachers need to know how to locate them (Ouzts 1994).

Previously mentioned, Rudman's book (1995) contains listings with annotations of books on many sensitive areas, such as divorce, death, adoption, foster care, family configurations, siblings, aging, abuse, sexuality, and special needs. Rasinski and Gillespie (1992) deal with some similar issues and also with drug and substance abuse issues, as well as dealing with the issue of "moving." Rudman, Gagne, and Bernstein

Activities for Uncovering Motivations and Practical Needs (Suggested for Younger Children)

1. Draw a picture of something you like to do.

2. Draw a picture of somebody you like to do it with. Who is it?

3. Draw a picture of something you would like to do, but don't know how to do it.

4. Draw a picture of somebody you would like to do it with.

5. Draw a picture of your whole family. Who is in the picture? Who do you like to do things with? What kind of things do you do?

(1994) focus entirely on books that have been selected to help children deal with "separation" and "loss." Finally, Friedberg, Mullins, and Suki-ennik (1992) and Robertson (1992) focus on nonfiction and fiction books that help children understand and promote their acceptance of a wide variety of physical, emotional, and medical disabilities.

Figure 6–3 Activities for uncovering motivations and practical needs (suggested for older elementary students)

Activities for Uncovering Motivations and Practical Needs (Suggested for Older Elementary Students)

Directions for the teacher: Older students could also draw or write their answers to these questions if they prefer not to pantomime.

1. Do you know how to do a pantomime? Pantomime is acting without words. Can you pantomime something you *like to do*, and we will try to guess what it is?

2. Can you pantomime something that you would like to *learn how to do*, and we will try to guess what it is?

3. Can you pantomime someone you like to, or would like to, do these things with? We will try to guess who it is.

4. If you could have three wishes to *change* anything, what would you change? Pantomime, and we will try to guess your wishes.

5. If you could have three wishes to *have* anything, what would you like to have? Pantomime, and we will try to guess your wishes.

Using readings in sensitive areas to help people understand and cope with special problems is known as bibliotherapy. Rudman (1995) indicates that the use of books to help children grapple with their personal problems has become accepted as an important part of teaching (2). She further states that using books to help children address these concerns is not putting teachers in the role of psychologists. Instead, she argues, because many children walk into today's classrooms grappling with many problems, and because teachers spend so much time with these children, teachers need to be competent to handle children's questions and concerns (2–3). However, Rudman warns that to be helpful, these book suggestions must not be prescribed or forced. Instead she suggests displaying books on a given theme and allowing children to discover them, recommending titles by posting them in an accessible area and having conferences where children and teachers feel comfortable sharing concerns and book ideas or suggestions.

Finally, Rudman has indicated that the teacher must always be sensitive to children's reactions. Ideally the reader should be able to identify with the character and action in the book. When teachers search for a variety of books to help children deal responsibly with the issue or problem, teachers should observe how the issue is treated; that is, books that provide "lessons to be learned" should be analyzed for their accuracy. The aesthetic quality of a book is still one of the most important factors to consider. Good children's literature can contain many issues and provide opportunities for students to deal with them. For example, Rudman explained that the death of Charlotte in E. B. White's *Charlotte's Web* (1952) helps readers understand and handle the concept of death while also providing a wonderful literary opportunity (3).

Appendix B of this book lists selected children's books dealing with some of the more common problems and areas of concern. These selections are presented just to give you an idea of the availability of books in sensitive areas. Teachers wanting more information, more books, and descriptions of each book should see Rudman (1995) or one of the other bibliographies available. (See Appendix A–7, "Literature to Help Children with Special Issues and Problems," for suggested bibliographies.) Additionally, when appropriate, and with the utmost sensitivity, teachers may be able to suggest some of these books to parents/families. However, care must be taken to not put the children in an embarrassing, awkward, or dangerous situation; and *if* it is deemed appropriate to share these book suggestions with parents/families, it is important that parents understand that the reading of the book must not be forced on their children.

Reflection Activity 6.2

How do you feel about using children's literature to assist children with their issues, concerns, problems, and needs? When do you feel it might be particularly appropriate?

Reading to "Do"

Have you ever read a "how-to-do-it" book? How to dress for success? How to refinish furniture? How to make and can preserves? How to travel cheaply? Many of us have read such material because we have a genuine desire to "do it ourselves,"—to dress right, to savor the fruits we picked this summer all year long, or to travel as much as we can afford. In other words, we were genuinely motivated.

If you have students who express an interest in a "learning-how-to" type of book or some other practical type of reading, encourage it. Reading for practical purposes is part of life. It is a tool we all need to succeed in life. Many adult basic education programs (programs for adults who need to further develop their basic literacy and other skills) stress this type of life-skill reading because of its essentiality in helping people to function in everyday life. For example, eventually almost everyone has to read a driver's manual to take their driving tests; people also need to read job applications, menus, cookbooks, and directions to do or to assemble specific things. These skills are "basic" to our literacy needs in the larger culture in which we live. Other literacy and how-to-do-it needs and motivations may also be basic to the diverse cultures and desires of your students and their families and immediate communities (Wlodkowski and Ginsberg [1995], emphasize that motivation is inseparable from culture). Give students the opportunities to read desired materials, and provide the help they may need locating desired materials. Often public librarians and various community agencies and businesses can be extremely helpful here.

As previously cautioned, mandating certain types and kinds of reading should not be a part of developing personal reading. Wait until your students express a real desire to read some specific how-to or other practical material before suggesting it. If it is appropriate, you and the student may also decide to involve the parent/family in this reading effort. Discussion regarding parent and family involvement will be addressed in Chapter 8.

Once they have the idea of what how-to-do-it books are, some students may want to make their own. In one second-grade class, I observed a flurry of bookmaking activity. See Figure 6–4 for a book on how to make blueberry pancakes by Octavia.

Figure 6–4   Second grader Octavia's how-to book on "cooking" blueberry pancakes

Figure 6–4 (Continued)

1. Firt you make playn pandcaks.
2. Mix them good!!!
3. Cok them good!!!
4. Dont' burn the pandcaks.!!!
5. Giv burnd pandcaks to the dog.
6. Put good pandcaks on playst.

(Continues)

Figure 6–4   (Continued)

7. Put the bluberezs on top.

8. Say com to the tabl the pandcaks are rede.

9. Eat them up.

10. Say do you lik them.

Evrebode Sayzs yes!!!

Reading for Practical Purposes: A Summary

This chapter presents some of the ways that students might read for practical purposes. These include reading to satisfy their motivations and special needs, reading to deal with various issues/problems and concerns, and reading to learn how to do something that is of importance to the student. The chapter also includes sample questions and activities that teachers could use to uncover students' motivations and other practical needs. Suggested questions and activities are provided to be used with older elementary students as well as with younger ones.

Try It Out

1. There are many points throughout the school day when students are curious to know more about a topic they are learning about, or wonder how something works. Perhaps one of them has just realized that if she could fix the old lawnmower in the garage, she could make extra money over the summer cutting grass for the neighbors. Encourage students to keep a journal or list in their desks in which they can record ideas like this. They can then use this journal as a basis for selecting reading materials for practical purposes.

2. Keep a current daily newspaper in a particular place in the classroom at all times. The answers to some of the questions students have may be found in its pages. It also happens to be a great way to get students in the habit of considering the daily newspaper as a good source of certain types of practical information.

3. Create a "Me, myself, and I" reading area where students can privately browse through books dealing with sensitive issues or problems. Have a variety of different books displayed and available in this corner dealing with many of the likely problems of students in your classroom. Be sure to also include nonfiction informational books as well as fictional trade books whose characters face challenges.

4. When discussing how-to-do-it books, point out the importance of following *all* instructions. What better way to demonstrate this than by inviting students to write their own? To begin, ask interested students to write directions on how to do something easy that they *know* how to do. For example, making a paper hat, setting the table correctly, or setting the classroom clock. Ask them to read the directions to a classmate who might want to know "how-to-do-it," and observe the classmate follow the directions. Do not add any steps that are not in the set of directions. See how well the directions instructed the classmate to complete the task.

Students who have some expertise in an area might enjoy writing and illustrating a how-to-do-it book for the benefit of others in the classroom. However, keep in mind that developing one's own personal literacy involves self-interest, self-choice, and self-motivation—and this goes for writing as well as reading—so don't push students into writing books if they don't *really* have a desire to do so.

7

Reading for Pleasure

What does so much of personal reading really seem to be all about? You guessed it: It is very often reading for pleasure or self-satisfaction. In most cases, if you really choose to read something and you are really motivated to read it, you will usually derive some sense of pleasure, accomplishment, or satisfaction from doing it. Clearly, all reading is not necessarily pleasurable, nor should it all be. I am not suggesting that. Even so, one of the primary aspects of personal reading should be the gaining of pleasure or satisfaction from one's reading. Again, remember the importance of the aesthetic stance (Rosenblatt 1978, 1991). Children should really get the message: "Reading is a pleasure!"

Evocative Books

Kurkjian and colleagues (2005) indicate that evocative books are books that inspire personal response and engagement. They are books that are so engaging they are difficult to put down. They are books that invite participation: books that allow readers to become so involved they can imagine themselves in the shoes of the characters; books that touch the lives of their readers in some way; books that compel readers to read them again and again; books that you don't want to end; books that linger with you long after you've finished reading them. Without a doubt, these are also books that invite reading for pleasure.

Reflection Activity 7.1

Have you read a book that fits this description? What is the name of the book and what made you love it so?

Wouldn't it be wonderful if all of our students could name books like that—books they continue to be drawn to, books they would rather read and engage with than do many other things? Teachers have the power to make this happen. In the sections that follow, suggestions are made that will help you facilitate the practice of reading for pleasure in your classroom.

Facilitating Reading for Pleasure

How do you facilitate extensive personal reading development in your classroom? How do you develop a desire to read for pleasure? There are many ways to facilitate these important values. First, you can create a comfortable, open, unstressful environment in your classroom so that your efforts to develop personal reading will meet with success. Second, you can provide the literate environment described herein, filling your room with a great variety of children's literature of good and good taste quality in many indicated interest areas, and frequently bring in new materials, replacing most books and magazines that have been around for more than two or three weeks. Third, you can model "reading is a pleasure" by allowing your children to see you really read and enjoy your own book every day. (Let them also see you taking it home to read and enjoy when not at school.) Fourth, you need to ensure that personal reading is a nonpunitive activity. Students must not be graded down or corrected for doing something "wrong." Instead, free-reading must be encouraged, honed, and nurtured. Reading for the sake of enjoyment, recreation, exploring interests, solving problems, or learning something new must be savored and honored. Fifth, you can read aloud to your students each and every day, selecting from their favorite books, or their suggested books, or some good literature you want to introduce. Finally, you can give children ample opportunity to share their own personal reading experiences with others, to suggest books to each other, and to write, when they wish, about their personal reading experiences.

Sharing Personal Reading: Its Importance

Children are often very excited and proud of their personal reading choices and accomplishments. Some children relish what they have learned, others relish "how many" books they have read, and others relish a particular story, character, or plot they came across in their personal reading. Sharing this excitement and these savored reading experiences is an extremely healthy way to achieve the goals of personal reading development. By sharing personal reading, children (1) can catch each other's enthusiasm about reading, (2) sometimes become interested in someone else's books, topics, and/or authors, and (3) often learn that reading can truly be a pleasure.

Of course, secondary benefits, which may really be primary benefits to other areas of your curriculum, are involved. During this sharing, students are often also enhancing their oral language skills, vocabulary skills, summarizing skills, analytic skills, critical skills, reporting skills, listening skills, writing skills, and, of course, their schemata in a wide variety of topics and areas.

Sharing Personal Reading: How To

Personal reading can be shared in a variety of ways. Several of these may be ones you already use in your classroom. Nevertheless, here are some possibilities that you can expand and embellish to fit your own style, perspective, philosophy, classroom, and students.

1. *Sharing through discussion.* Students can form small literature circles or discussion and sharing groups to discuss one or more books each week or as often as possible. You will need to allow the group to pace itself based on the students' selections and available times. The Roser and Martinez (1995) book is especially recommended to help you with "book talk" ideas and to facilitate "book talk" discussions.

2. *Sharing through writing.* Students can keep response journals or literature logs of their personal readings. Many literacy educators suggest these types of journals, logs and other writing about reading (but *not* book reports, please), as a means of creating opportunities for students to reflect on, react to, and make memorable the books they have read (e.g., see Angelillo 2003; Hancock 1993). (A note to readers: Literacy experts all agreed that requiring a book report of every book that students read would *not* be a good practice [Flippo 2001, 1999, 1998].)

   Students can also be encouraged to respond to suggested questions like the following: What did you like best about this book? How does this book fulfill your expectations about it? Are there any particular ideas you'd like to discuss that relate to this book? Teachers can ask students to share their responses to these questions, or any other reflections students would like to share about a book, with the teacher and with other students by writing in their dialogue journals. Nash (1995) has pointed out the benefits of this type of personal reflection, sharing, and ongoing dialogue through writing.

   Whatever type of journal writing you suggest for your students' use, keep in mind that the purpose of this writing is to allow students to think and feel about what they have read and give them opportunities to share these thoughts and feelings in a meaningful way for each of them (Handloff and Golden 1995).

3. *Sharing through drama, art, music, and dance.* Galda and West (1995) have suggested sharing all kinds of books through use of dramatizations. Fennessey (1995) has proposed the sharing of historical readings and enhancing understandings of these readings through use of drama, music, and dance. Zarrillo (1994) has suggested many ideas for sharing literature through various performing

and visual arts projects. Zarrillo's ideas include using drama, song, and dance. He also has suggested use of puppets, Readers' Theater, bulletin board displays, dioramas (three-dimensional displays), and collages (combinations of various materials, cut and pasted) to represent children's feelings about their readings. Zarrillo has noted that these sharing activities (including others, like journal writing) are excellent for including and working with learners from all diverse cultural backgrounds. Galda and Cullinan (2006) also have recommended that children make character puppets and put on their own puppet shows as a creative and fun way to share their special books with other children.

Following are other art, drama, and music/dance ideas I have used and particularly like.

- Children can create whole wall murals displaying the most interesting and exciting characters and parts of their favorite books.
- Students can pantomime representations of their favorite books and play "book charades," where children get to act out book titles and plots and other students must guess which book they are representing.
- Children can develop a musical background for their special books, creating a tape of mood or action music to go with the reading of a book, or with special parts of the book.
- Children can create dances to show the relationship of characters in their favorite books or to show the passage of time or special events.

Obviously, different kinds of sharing and different drama, art, and music/dance options are more appropriate to some books than to others. Some children also prefer using certain mediums over others. Children should always be free to share in ways they feel are most appropriate to their particular books and their particular preferences. Also, if children do not want to share, they have the right to not do so. Again these should all be personal choices for personal reading.

4. *Sharing through recommendations.* Students may want to make recommendations about books they have read and share these with others in their class. These recommendations can be done orally or in writing. For instance, I have seen classrooms where students do

"bookselling" fairs, displaying and "selling" the reading of their favorite books to one another. Or some teachers suggest that students write their recommendations about a book and put it on a card in the book jacket or pocket so that other students will have opportunities to review their peers' recommendations before selecting a book.

5. *Sharing through annotations.* Students can develop their own, or group, or whole-class annotated bibliographies. Students could develop lists providing the full citations of a book followed by a short summary. These lists can be done topically to create a continuous source of available readings categorized by interest area or topics for the use of other students, the teacher, and the teacher's future classes. Using classroom computers, the students could use a database program (e.g., Microsoft Works or AppleWorks) to compile, store, and manipulate their annotations by author, topic, and interest among other variables. Both you and interested students could then be given a hard copy of the book annotations available and stored on the database on particular interest areas and topics.

Reflection Activity 7.2

How do you or could you give children the message that "reading is a pleasure"? How do you encourage children to share their special treasured books? How do you give a child the message that what he thinks really counts and is important, while also stimulating other children to want to read a special book?

Where Are These Treasured Books?

These memorable and often treasured books, which children love, are *all over!* While no one can say that all children, or even a particular child, will love a specific book, we have seen that many children's books are truly loved by many children, and the titles of these books are cited in the literature again and again. For instance, Kurkjian and colleagues (2005) name and describe many of these books. Each year, in coordination with the Children's Book Council (CBC), *The Reading Teacher*, an International Reading Association (IRA) journal, publishes in its October issue a list of the previous year's best-loved books—some for each age group. Many of these are categorized for you in Appendix B of this book. Many authors of professional books of children's literature for teachers also cite these and other books—these sources are also provided for you in Appendix A.

It is important to remember, however, that loving something, or someone, is in the eyes of the beholder. A child may just love a book that few others exalt. What is important is that *the child loves the book* and wants to read it for pleasure, again and again. This is what we are after! The popularity of a book is really not the important thing. Here's an example:

When my son, Todd, was between two and five years old, he *loved* the books *A Fish out of Water* (1961) by Helen Palmer, and *The Mellops Go Spelunking* (1963) and *The Mellops Go Flying* (1957) by Tomi Ungerer. He asked me to read those three books to him over and over again, and, of course, I did. He enjoyed reading them on his own as well. Although Todd had numerous books that he enjoyed, he truly loved and treasured those three. It was actually upsetting to me recently when I tried to purchase them for Todd's daughter Elena, that the Ungerer books were out of print. Obviously, even though Todd adored the Mellops (a wonderful, adventurous, and creative family of pigs), it seemed that interest in them was not universal—I also do not remember seeing a mention of these three books he so loved on any listings of books loved by children. Loving a book, you see, is a very personal thing at any age—and it is the most important thing.

The next chapter discusses the foundation of personal reading (or the "umbrella handle" as depicted in Figure 1–1): culture, family, and community. This foundation has the greatest influence on children's personal reading motivations and pursuits. Because of this, it is extremely important for teachers to understand these influences and work with parents, families, and the community to connect the personal reading development we are attempting to do in school with the children's real lives and cultures outside of school.

Elena (age 3) and Grandpa (Papa) sharing and loving a book.

Reading for Pleasure: A Summary

This chapter discusses reading for pleasure, facilitating this type of reading, the importance of reading for pleasure, sharing of personal reading, and where to find books that children will truly love. The emphasis is that as teachers we should want children and older students to find reading a pleasure. We want children to love reading special, memorable books. These books do not have to be everyone's favorite books. What is important is that the reader has an opportunity to get pleasure out of the books he or she chooses, and learns that reading can be a great pleasure.

Zoe (age 2) and Grandma (author) sharing and loving a book.

Try It Out

1. Have interested children work in groups of two or three to create commercials for either a favorite book, or for reading for pleasure in general. Give them the time and the support needed to create a commercial with a script, props, and signs. If you have a camcorder for audio-video recording, try using that. Also, you can make a stage area in your classroom and allow the groups to perform the commercials for each other. This will enable students to discover together what is enjoyable about reading, and present it to their peers.

2. Have a "reading party" afternoon. One Friday, bring in many blankets and sleeping bags to school. Tell children in advance that they may bring a favorite stuffed animal and some books from home. On Friday afternoon, move the desks to the perimeter of the classroom and lay out the pillows, sleeping bags, and blankets around the classroom floor. Also, put many books out around the classroom on desks and tables to display them and make them accessible and inviting (as is done in bookstores). Have children get comfortable on the floor and read for pleasure for a certain amount of time. Then take a break and do a teacher read-aloud. Following the read-aloud, allow children to read in pairs. If allowed by the school, provide some juice and cookies or fruit for the children to snack on. This reading party should certainly get kids excited about reading for fun!

3. We all want our students to recognize that reading can be enjoyable. Talk to them about books you enjoyed as a child. Read one or two of them to the class if they are interested. Display these books in the classroom library for children to read if they choose.

    If children are interested in talking about the books that were their favorites when they were younger, give them the opportunity to do so. It is important for them to share their literary experiences and talk about books that they love.

Perhaps some of the children can find photographs at home, or at grandma's house, of themselves reading a book, or someone else reading a book to them, when they were younger. Ask them to bring those photos in and share them with the class. Perhaps they can develop a bulletin board for the photos and write about what they might have been reading or thinking about when the picture was taken—and/or who was reading to them.

4. Create a pen-pal or email-buddy partnership with a class from another school in your area or in another part of the country. Have the students share with their buddy favorite books they have read, what the books are about, and why the students like them.

5. If you and your students want more ideas for Readers' Theater, take a look at the website www.aaronshep.com/rt. This site provides resources including free scripts by children's author Aaron Shepard.

Culture, Family, and Community Connections

8

To a great extent, teachers control the activities and climate of personal reading endeavors in school. The teacher's encouragement, praise, and presence are often a catalyst for some children who may not otherwise participate. However, the personal reading that students engage in outside school is a different matter. To ensure that personal reading development efforts are maximized for each child in the classroom, the teacher must take certain steps to make very necessary and important cultural, family, and community connections both in and out of the classroom. In this chapter, each of these connections is discussed.

Cultural Connections

The professional literature abounds with books, research, and discussions emphasizing the importance of children's culture and diverse backgrounds and how these must be used to plan instruction and learning activities for children of all ages (e.g., Block and Zinke 1995, Díaz-Rico and Weed 2006, Gonzalez-Mena 2005, Opitz 1998, Pang 2005, Lewis 1996, Tiedt and Tiedt 2005, Wlodkowski and Ginsberg 1995, and Zarrillo 1994). Of course, development of students' personal reading is a part of all of this.

Throughout this book, I have emphasized the importance of meeting the interests, motivations, real needs, prior knowledge, and diversities of all learners. Now, consider the following culturally responsive teaching conditions, developed and depicted by Wlodkowski and Ginsberg (1995) and further developed and summarized by me to fit the purposes of this book.

1. Teachers must find ways of including all students in the learning activities. (This means classroom teachers must emphasize the human purpose of what is being read and relate it to students' personal experience. They can do this by engaging students in cooperative and collaborative activities; treating all students equally and with respect; and using approaches that facilitate the personal reading development of diverse students, including use of shared reading and writing groups, interest groups, cooperative learning, and ways of sharing that can include art, drama, music/dance, and other personal-choice ways of sharing personal reading.)

2. Teachers must find ways of developing the positive attitudes of all students. (This means classroom teachers can help students relate reading choices to their experiences, motivations, interests, and prior knowledge. Students must be encouraged to make their own choices in their book selections. Teachers must be flexible in teaching styles, allow for individualization, and accept students' current developing personal reading. One approach that can facilitate these positive attitudes is *matching the interests and motivations of all learners* to the reading selections.)

3. Teachers must find ways of enhancing meaning for all students. (This means classroom teachers must provide appropriate pre- and post-reading experiences that will challenge students to use higher-order thinking and critical inquiry. Teachers must address the real issues and real concerns of the world in which we live and relate those to the very important world of each student. Reflections and discussions, classroom dialogue, and sharing of ideas are to be encouraged. Teachers can help students find meaningful books,

texts, and materials for reading, written in meaningful language, and with relevant and meaningful discussion. Approaches that can facilitate the enhancement of meaning include critical questioning, students' decision making, and sharing their own research and project-type learning.)

4. Teachers must find ways of encouraging the competence of all students in their personal reading pursuits as well as in their other literacy-related work in school. (This means classroom teachers must use appropriate, multiple, and authentic assessments to find out about students' strategies, skills, needs, motivations, and interests. Teachers must then build on those existing strategies and interests/motivations to help students develop other strategies that are necessary for success in school and society. Assessments and instruction must be connected with students' desires to succeed and accomplish. Teachers must accept and appreciate differences, and appreciate growth when it takes place. And students must be given opportunities to reflect on and self-assess their own development, work, and progress. Approaches that can facilitate the encouraging of competence include portfolio assessment, authentic assessment, self-assessment, individual conferences and feedback, narrative evaluations as opposed to grades, and individualized instruction.)

Cultural Diversity

What is meant by cultural diversity? What is really involved? And how does cultural diversity impact your school? These are important questions to consider as you plan for cultural connections with students, their families, and communities.

Let's take a look at one scenario of a culturally diverse classroom in a Massachusetts community to see some examples of cultural diversity. I've called the school Neighborhood School, and the community is Center Towne. Ms. Lee is the teacher, and she herself is second-generation Chinese American. She has been fortunate to get this combination first- and second-grade teaching position because jobs have been especially hard to find in this part of Massachusetts for the past few years; however, her own cultural heritage and her ability to speak fluent English, as well as to fluently speak two different dialects of Chinese, were particularly helpful in attaining the position. Ms. Lee's fluency in Chinese will be especially useful because she has four children of Chinese ethnicity in her classroom who are in various stages of learning English and who speak different Chinese dialects. Her other students include: three Laotian Americans, two Cambodian Americans, five African Americans, two Vietnamese Americans, four European Americans, and three Latinos (two newly from El Salvador, and one from Guatemala, who has been in the United States since he was a toddler). Needless to say, their ethnicity, cultures, languages, community identifications, and religions are quite diverse!

Ms. Lee wants to provide quality education for all of her students. She has many who are in the process of acquiring English as a second language. She also knows that these children, even though of similar ages, have various differences regarding their literacy development, linguistic and cognitive strategies, cognitive abilities, special needs, prior experiences, and interests and motivations. She plans to facilitate their personal reading development and other literacy learning by getting to know each of her students' interests, motivations, strengths, and needs, and by using various materials, instructional strategies, and motivations to help them develop as readers, writers, and learners in her classroom. Because of the cultural diversity of her classroom, school, and community (Center Towne), Ms. Lee plans to use the entire community (parents, families, and other community members) as much as possible to reach her goals for these students.

To help her get started, Ms. Lee gathers professional literature that she will use as a resource to help inform her instruction. For instance, she uses *Buddy Reading* (Samway, Whang, and Pippitt 1995) to help her develop ideas for a cross-age tutoring program between her classroom and another classroom in Neighborhood School. She uses Harris' (1997) book, *Using Multiethnic Literature in the Grades K–8 Classroom* (and many other sources cited in Appendix A–6), to locate children's literature from a variety of cultures representative of children in her classroom. She also reads books and articles on multicultural education, multicultural literacy, and culturally responsive teaching that include Banks (2002); Boyd, Brock, and Rozendal (2004); Cary (2000); Gersten and Jiménez (1994); and Wlodkowski and Ginsberg (1995).

Using the Cultural Difference Model

So, what ideas and model will Ms. Lee use to accomplish her goals when there is so much diversity in her classroom? Well, one idea that especially appeals to her is the cultural difference model (Banks 2002). Because she herself had firsthand experience, as a child in school, of negative expectations (or a cultural-deficit model), Ms. Lee believes that a model that respects each child's differences and uses those differences as positive materials to enrich the classroom would be just right for her very diverse classroom and students. The ideas of this model, and specifically what Ms. Lee believes are: (1) the school and the teacher, not the cultures of the students, are responsible for low academic achievement; (2) the school and the teacher must change in ways that will result in respect for all students and teaching strategies that are consistent with students' cultural characteristics; (3) teaching strategies will be culturally sensitive and enriched to enable students to achieve; (4) the school and teacher will not ignore or try to alienate students from their cultures but instead use their cultures in positive ways; and (5) the school and teacher will view other languages spoken by their students as strengths, rather than as problems to overcome (Banks 2002).

Reflection Activity 8.1

Cultural diversity is more and more part of all of our lives and is part of school experience. What does cultural diversity mean to you as a teacher, and how have you used it in positive ways in your classroom? Specifically, how could you use cultural diversity to enhance the personal reading development of your students?

It is obvious that culturally responsive teachers like Ms. Lee understand that students' cultures and backgrounds need to be honored and respected. Teachers clearly need to meet with, work with, and learn from the students' parents, families, and communities. They, and the students themselves, are the teacher's greatest resource for assessing and successfully working with each child. The next sections explore some parent/family and community connection ideas that I hope will help facilitate the development of every child's personal reading.

Parent/Family Connections

The importance of working with students' parents and families is well recognized. Many educators have emphasized and called for more attention to developing and respecting these connections (e.g., Berger 2004; DeBruin-Parecki and Krol-Sinclair 2003; Lilly and Green 2004; Morrow 1995; Rasinski 1995; Shockley 1994; Shockley, Michalove, and Allen 1995; and Taylor 1997). Working with parents/families now involves much more than just having parent conferences, or sending letters home. Today when we talk about making parent/family connections and working with parents/families, we are usually talking about collaborating with parents/families, learning about each child and each child's literacy history from them, and involving parents/families in children's assessment and instruction decisions. For instance, in *Assessing Readers* (Flippo 2003) I devise questions and ideas for gathering information from parents about their child's literacy development and strategies and their family literacy practices. I also suggest ways of involving parents/families in three-way reciprocal conferences (parent, child, and teacher), with each member having equal say-so and power, to assess progress and plan future outcomes. Additionally, I expand and discuss new ideas for sharing report card evaluations and other home–school communications. This kind of parent/family involvement in assessment and instruction and continuous collaboration can foster the development of students' personal reading. In Figure 8–1 (see also Appendix D), drawing on three-way reciprocal conferencing and sharing of ideas (Flippo 2003, 233–36), I tailor a format for the sharing of personal reading development information.

Parents and other family members must know that they play *the* essential role in their child's literacy and personal reading development. Teachers need to continue to make connections with their students' families, because parents' attitudes about reading do affect children's attitudes toward reading (Shockley 1994). Parents need to know what is going on in the school curricula and how they can be involved and help their child to learn (Flippo and Smith 1990). Parents also can be encouraged to help their child find literature that meets their child's interests, desires, and needs. They can take part in their child's personal reading

Figure 8–1 Three-way reciprocal conferencing: Sharing personal reading information and ideas

Three-Way Reciprocal Conferencing: Sharing Personal Reading Information and Ideas

Date	Child's first and last name	Grade
My thoughts regarding the accomplishments of our sharing	My/our thoughts regarding the accomplishments of our sharing	My thoughts regarding the accomplishments of our sharing
[Child's name]	[Family member's name(s)]	[Teacher's name]

Plans for personal reading:

development by sharing literature with their child, and encouraging special times each evening for family reading opportunities.

Parents/family should be encouraged to read aloud to their children of all ages. In Figure 8–2, I recommend specific steps for parents/family members to follow when reading a book to their child. You might share

How to Read a Book to Your Child

Reading a book to your child should be a pleasant experience for both of you, a time you and your child can relish together. Use the following list of steps only as a guide to help you and your child develop your own unique way of sharing books.

1. Carefully select a book for your child from a selection of good children's books. Or select several books and let the child choose one from the group. Or allow your child to independently select a book. (It is probably best to alternate your methods of selecting a book to be read from the three ways suggested, but when your child *wants* you to read a particular book, please honor her request.)

2. Talk about the book before you begin to read it so that your youngster knows the title, is familiar with the cover, and has been told the author's name. This will allow the child to anticipate the book. This will also help the child realize that someone wrote the book and that a book is someone else's thoughts, ideas, and talk written down.

3. Read the book to your child, stopping often to point at or talk about different things in the pictures, according to the child's interests. (But remember, throughout the reading, you are *not teaching* the book, you want this experience to be relaxing and very pleasurable for your child.)

4. As you read the book, ask questions that your child can answer by looking for clues in the pictures or making inferences from what has already been read. Allow your child time to answer, and praise your child's comments whenever possible. If you disagree with the answer, ask your youngster about it. If the answer is not at all applicable, talk about other possible answers to the same question. Be careful not to say, "That's wrong," "You didn't understand," or "No, that's not right."

5. After you have read the book, talk about things in the book with which your child is familiar, or things in which the child is interested. Encourage your youngster to talk about the book.

6. Occasionally, allow your child an opportunity to illustrate a favorite part of the book after you have finished reading it. Sometimes let the child verbalize the theme of the book to you as you write down the child's exact words; then display them with the picture.

7. Very often your child will want to read a favorite book to you. Allow this whenever possible. *Do not correct errors.* The child is not reading words but is retelling the story from memory. This gives you a chance to observe the progress of your child's oral language and memory development. This practice and opportunity will be very good, providing that you are supportive and don't turn this into a reading lesson.

Elena's and Zoe's Mommy reading to them.

Grandpa (Papa) reading to Elena and Zoe.

this and other foundational literacy development information with parents/family and, when possible, demonstrate it for them in your classroom. Be sure to emphasize flexibility and the need for this experience to be loving and pleasant for the parent(s), the grandparent(s), or other family members with the child(ren). A wonderful photo is shown on the previous page of Elena, age three, and Zoe, age eighteen months, enjoying a book experience with Mommy (our daughter-in-law, Jen), as she reads a book to them. You also see Tyler, my husband, and their Grandpa (otherwise known as Papa), lovingly reading to Elena and Zoe. Even older sisters or brothers can read to younger children. On the next page, at 3½, Elena reads a bedtime book to Zoe, now 2. Finally, Grandma (me) gets an opportunity to read to the girls.

Teachers planning to involve parents and families in their children's personal reading development might want to consider the following relevant ideas. Goodman and Haussler (1986) suggested beliefs that still serve as a classroom point of reference from which to proceed:

1. All families offer children knowledge of reading and writing—just the forms are different.

2. Having all kinds of reading and writing matter easily accessible to children is an important aspect of literacy development.

3. Attitudes expressed by family members in the home toward reading and writing have an impact on children's learning.

4. Children learn language that is meaningful and functional to them.

5. Children should not be penalized by the school for coming from a home where more practical, less literary forms of reading and writing are valued and used.

6. Children's oral language and the extension of what they already know about literacy should be the foundation on which school reading and writing programs are built.

Older sisters can read to younger ones. Here's Elena (at 3½), reading to Zoe (2).

Grandma (author) reading to Elena and Zoe.

Community Connections

Transitions from home connections to community connections involve only subtle differences. Additionally, research indicates that strong family and community connections with their children's classrooms lead to students who achieve more in school (Nieto 2004). Children and their families and homes are part of the larger sociocultural community in which they live. Children and their families cannot be understood if treated apart from this community.

For example, here's another scenario: Danling, a Laotian child, and her family live in a housing complex that is composed of families representing various diverse cultures. However, a large percentage of these families do come from several Asian Pacific cultures. Danling's family is involved in activities of their church, and when time permits, they take part in neighborhood meetings, activities, and celebrations. Although, Danling has to go home to an empty apartment every day after school because her parents work two jobs and do not get home until late in the evening, Danling's immediate community provides for her safety and well-being in her parents' absence. In fact, Danling often eats dinner at her friend's apartment and does her homework over there. She also spends a great deal of time at another friend's house down the street. The influence and connections between Danling and her immediate community (her family, her friend Kim's family, her friend Chiang's family, her church family, and her neighborhood) are complex, but important. These connections and influences must be part of the teacher's efforts to work with Danling. Because Danling's parents are only part of her community, her teacher, Miss Jackson, works at including and involving the other community members in Danling's personal reading development whenever possible. After all, Danling spends much of her awake hours with these other community members. Their beliefs, their attitudes, and their ideas will have an influence on Danling.

Additionally, it is also helpful to view the child as a member of his immediate community. As a member of this community, a child often must be involved in community life, concerns, and affairs. For example, if a child's community is in a volatile area that has been feeling unsafe to the child's family and neighbors, it is likely that issues involving safety are currently very important in that community. These issues may need to also be dealt with in school if the child is to see school as part of her real life. These issues may become part of the child's personal reading concerns and interests and should be honored if they are.

Community connections also include community agencies, businesses, intergenerational programs, and services that can aid teachers in their personal reading development efforts with students. For example, many community agencies are available to help with specific problems and needs. Many community businesses are delighted to get involved and help out by coming to your classroom to share ideas and materials, by donating books and materials, and by serving as a resource in various areas of expertise. Intergenerational programs can be developed between your school, or your classroom, and older community members, or perhaps even retirement residences in your community. Arrangements can be made for these senior citizens to read aloud to children in your class. Perhaps your students could also go to an assisted-living or a nursing home and read aloud to seniors who may no longer be able to read on their own. Community services like those provided by the public library can often supplement what your school library does not have. Take advantage of these connections and use them all you can. Also be respectful of these connections; perhaps you and your students can think of ways to help these agencies, businesses, senior citizens, and services in some way to reciprocate for the help they provide to you.

Professional books, research, and writings have been looking at these and other community connections (e.g., Flippo et al. 1997; Morrow 1995; Morrow, Tracey, and Maxwell 1995; Risko and Bromley 2001; and Rowe and Probst 1995 will provide you with a small sampling). Think about your students' communities; connections you can make with them; the resources they can bring into your classroom; and ways you can consider and weave the students' immediate community needs, values, and issues into your classroom curricula and life.

Drawing on my own ideas and also on the insightful questions raised by Bromley and Risko (2001), I developed a "Community Connections Think-About List" (Figure 8–3) to illustrate one of the ways you can list and consider the possible connections available to you. Because every community is unique, and every group of children and their teachers must decide for themselves how they can help and how they can use some help, I've left lots of room for you to add your own

Figure 8–3   Community connections think-about list

Community Connections Think-About List

Connections to make	Resources for our students	Resources we can offer
Public library	After-school summer reading programs and activities	Students volunteer to come early and help librarian
Mayor's office		
Senior center		
Assisted-living complex		
YMCA		
YWCA		
Bookstores		
Fire station		
Police station		
Recycling center		
City newspaper office		
"Summer Fun" book reading program		
Children's museum		
Local book authors		
City "Project Bread"		

connections, resources to share, and resource needs appropriate to your particular community and class situation. In Appendix D–3 you will find a skeleton checklist that you and your students can examine and fill in together, as you develop your ideas for the *real* community connections you envision over time.

Reflection Activity 8.2

How important do you feel that culture, family, and community connections are to your students' personal reading selections and development? How might you explain this to your school administrator, or to a school board member in your district?

Culture, Family, and Community Connections: A Summary

This chapter looks at the importance of children's culture, family, and community, and how these relate to the development of their personal reading, as well as to their interests, motivations, and needs. Scenarios are shared to clarify cultural diversity in the classroom, and family and community influences on each child. The chapter discusses making connections by meeting and working with family and community members as well as the child, and gives examples of various possible connections. Additionally, a checklist is provided to help teachers use all the community connections available to them.

Try It Out

1. As this chapter has indicated, it is very important to keep in mind culture, family, and community connections as they relate to personal reading. Have each child invite parents, family, and other relevant community members to class for a Reading and Sharing Celebration, where each student who would like to participate shares something from a special book they have chosen to read and enjoy. Some students may wish to share pictures they particularly liked in the book, or tell about something funny or interesting from the book, or simply hold up the book and say, "This is a book I *really* liked!" Family and community guests are likewise invited to bring a book or story that they would like to share with the children at this celebration.

2. Find out about and encourage your students to attend programs at local libraries, after school, on weekends, and during vacations. Most offer a host of activities that parents, family members, and caregivers can take children to. They may offer puppet shows, folktales, music and dance, all incorporated into a literacy theme. Check out your local library, make the needed connections, and try it out!

3. Work closely with youth-service groups, local bookstores, senior centers, assisted-living complexes, and community organizations within the school's community to support school and non-school reading opportunities. Design projects to involve your students in reading activities with seniors, after-school and holiday programs, free-book programs, and other activities; these projects will benefit not only your students but also those in the community whose lives they touch.

4. Teachers and parents should have continuous conversations about "reading for meaning" and ways to motivate each student to be an active reader both inside and outside school. With your encouragement and initial help in planning, perhaps a group of students and

parents might launch a children's book club designed to encourage reading on a personal level, and facilitated by several parents in the same locality; a club that could serve as a venue where children periodically meet and talk with their peers about their favorite books. The parents would be there as facilitators; their children as literate persons who share and discuss books. Follow-up activities to the book discussions can include art, drama, dance, and music— projects that allow children to act out favorite parts of their books, draw or print characters from their books, make posters or murals to advertise their books, and develop a dance or song that shows the mood or feelings portrayed in their books. Juice and cookie refreshments would be a perfect happy ending for each club meeting.

5. Celebrate National Children's Book Week! Each year, The Children's Book Council (CBC) sponsors this special week during the week prior to Thanksgiving. CBC can be contacted in advance for ideas and activities to share and publicize the fun of reading with your students, their families, and communities. Involve all of them in your celebration of the joy of books. Make this special week a yearly event for your classroom. The address of the CBC can be found in Appendix A–1.

Afterword

hroughout this book I share my definition of personal reading, which involves students' self-motivated behavior to select and read from materials in areas that can include their current interests, new and developing interests, recreational readings, academic interests, practical readings, and pursuits of pleasure. To promote the personal reading development of each student, I also include my ideas concerning use of interest, motivation, and other relevant questions, as well as examples of ways that teachers can use children's interests, purposes, and diverse cultures within the classroom curriculum and for their classroom planning.

To me, each aspect of personal reading is important, and the reading of all "good taste" literature as well as "good" literature is to be valued. The development of each child's personal reading will be enhanced when the child's culture, family, and community are all considered and respected.

At the end of this book, in the appendixes, I provide a comprehensive listing of professional references and resources to assist you in the continual search for "good taste" literature and "good" literature that meets students' interests, needs, and purposes. Also included is a sampling of children's literature suggestions taken from a few of these professional resources. Together, these provide an idea of the scope of what is available. Keep in mind that updated professional resources and new children's literature are published each year. By checking the references and resources I've provided, you'll be able to stay aware of new offerings.

I hope you have seen that students' personal reading pursuits can often be applied to early childhood and elementary curricula and classrooms in interesting and motivating ways. But I also hope you will remember that personal reading must always involve students' self-motivation and self-selection and *should not ever be forced.*

As a mother of two children, Todd and Tara, and now as a grandmother of two "little ones" (Elena and Zoe), I can tell you that along with their health and happiness, I have always hoped for the love and pursuit of personal reading for each of them. I am thankful for their fulfillment of my hopes and wish the same for your family and the children you teach.

More Try It Out Activities

1. Children love to have their opinion valued. Provide a section in your reading corner(s) for students to place books on display that they would highly recommend to other students.

2. A great reading experience in a classroom is to hold a book club meeting. Using a book that all students are comfortable with, facilitate a book club discussion and encourage students to voice *their* opinions about the book's plot, characters, and setting. Bring in snacks and have the meeting on a rug or in a comfortable reading corner or area. (Let the children decide where.) Allow this to be a very pleasurable and relaxing experience for them.

3. Create a student-operated paperback bookshop. A paperback bookshop can be set up in any school. If space is available, a small room makes an excellent bookshop. If space is a problem, books can be stored in portable book carts and set up in cafeterias or wherever else students congregate. Students select, shelve, price, and market the books, which gives them an opportunity to make books more accessible to other students. Suggest that the profits be used to purchase more inventory for bookshop sales.

4. If you teach in an upper grade, invite your students to go to the library to find books they liked when they were younger. Arrange with primary grade teachers to have your students read and talk about these books with children in their classrooms, explaining why they picked each book and what they liked about it. Your students would benefit from the opportunity to share and model their reading—building self-esteem and appreciation of a good story. This would likewise help alert younger readers to the fact that many of these stories and books have been around a long time, and that bigger kids like to read them. (Many "little ones," for example, my three-and-a-half-year-old granddaughter Elena, like to think of themselves as "big." Part of being a big girl or boy is doing things that big kids do.)

5. Play soft, soothing classical music during SSR, or during other free-reading time. Try it out! Ask your students if the music enhanced their reading experience. Ask how? If any of the students felt that the music was disruptive to their reading, use it as an opportunity to talk about the ideal reading setting, and of course, do not use music in future sessions.

6. Be your favorite author's character. The children and the teacher(s) (and other school staff, too, if they wish to participate) could come to school dressed up as their favorite storybook character. You could arrange for a parade in the classroom (or the auditorium, if it is a schoolwide event). This would help make everyone aware of different books that are available and might stimulate children to become interested in reading particular books because their characters evoke a sense of curiosity.

7. With young children, you may want to try reading aloud a familiar story while having some of the students act out the scenes. You could have several renditions as you alter the tone and voice used to read the story. By using familiar stories, such as "The Three Little Pigs," the audience usually knows what to expect and the actors have a chance to inject their interpretations of the reading.

8. Design an inviting, eye-appealing "Our Genre and Topics" book-shelf or special space with the children. Include multiple types of reading materials of various topics and genres. Make sure the children have a say in the design, setup, selection of material, and in the running of their space (inventory, check-out policies, etc.).

9. Try out books on tape and e-books with your class. Books on tape can be used by a class as they read along silently, or by an individual child with a set of headphones. Books on tape can also be an occasional alternative to the teacher reading aloud to the class. The Internet also offers many children's Websites that promote reading through e-book selections. Some of these include:

www.pbskids.org   www.funschool.com
www.berensteinbears.com   www.suessville.com
www.mattlescrabble.com   www.scholastic.com
www.kidsdomain.com   www.sesameworkshop.org
www.literacycenter.net   www.janbrett.com

10. Take a classic piece of children's literature, such as *Charlotte's Web* (1952) by E. B. White, and rewrite it into a short, scaled-down version lacking warmth, depth, interesting characters, dialogue, story line, sensitivity, and descriptive details. For example, "Wilbur is a pig. He meets Charlotte and some other barnyard animals. Wilbur likes Charlotte. Wilbur is sad when Charlotte dies." After they read *Charlotte's Web*, read them the scaled-down version you prepared and ask which version of the story they enjoyed more, and why. Develop this into a discussion on what makes a book a "good book."

11. Students can make a reading review card for each book they read. These can be alphabetized and kept in a box (a shoe box could work) for other students' reference near the classroom reading corner(s) or area. Multiple students can write reviews of the same book. What was enjoyable for one student may not be enjoyable for another.

Title:

Author:

Illustrator:

Publisher:

Summary:

Genre:

Do you recommend this book? Why?

Reviewer's name (student's name):

12. It is helpful for students to understand the qualities they consider to be a part of a "good book." Have students make a list of qualities of good books they have read. Continue to update these lists as the school year goes on.

13. When studying an academic unit, there is usually an academic text that is used, but also try to find other types of reading that could be used to complement the unit. Trade books have been written for *so many* topics of interest and study. Some examples of this would be selections of the Magic School Bus series for science topics on butterflies, magnets, the solar system, electricity and many more. For historical units, the Magic Tree House series has many selections on subjects such as the Civil War, ancient Olympics and many other historical events or time periods. These can be shared with

students as teacher read-alouds, or they can be left on display in the class reading area for students to read as they wish.

14. When working on a particular area of content interest, invite students to get into small groups according to their major interest and create a book for the classroom library on the particular topic. The children would need to pick out key points, summarize, write content, edit, and produce. They can get the information for the research project from the classroom text, other books, encyclopedias (online or printed) and the Internet.

15. The World Wide Web is a rich source for visual images, texts, and audio and video clips on a wide variety of topics, subjects, and interests. Students can explore particular sites based on a topic of study or a particular area that they want to research. Students can do research independently or in groups (if they have similar motivations or interests). This allows students the opportunity to pursue their interests with others who share these interests, prepare reports and other sharings collaboratively, and also use various multiple media resources to make the information more interesting for all concerned.

16. For young children, introduce "how-to-do-it" books with a fun activity. For instance, you can have children volunteer to tell you *exactly* how to make a jelly sandwich. Prepare the scene by putting some bread, a knife, a plate, and the jelly on a table or a desk at the front of the room. Then ask them to give you precise, step-by-step instructions for making the sandwich. Write these on the board, and carry them out literally. For example, if a child says, "Put the jelly on the bread," then physically put the jar of jelly on top of the bread.

   Use this fun activity to teach children about the importance of detail and specificity in "how-to-do-it" books. Following the activity, introduce a new crate of how-to books for the classroom, and show a few of them to the children. Then have a brainstorming session where interested children decide what they could put into a how-to-do-it book themselves. Encourage those who *really want* to do it to write and present their own how-to books.

17. To emphasize the importance of reading for pleasure, the teacher could share her favorite books with the students. If students see how

passionate the teacher is about reading, it should motivate them to "want to read."

Continue to encourage independent reading time each day, with both the students and teacher taking part in this. After this, you could formulate a large circle where everyone has the opportunity to share with the class favorite parts of their books. If needed to promote sharing, the teacher can prompt discussion about characters, setting, theme, and the "feeling" that the students took away from the book.

18. Book buddies are a great way of giving older English language learners in the community an opportunity to try out their language skills by reading easy text to your developing readers. The older community members benefit by successfully reading a book to your students and gain confidence from reading aloud. You and your younger students benefit through the community and cultural connections you make, as well as the extra help and attention your students get in the classroom.

19. Organize a reading workshop for parents and family members. Share and demonstrate suggestions for how parents can encourage their children to further develop personal reading at home. Entice the parents to attend by having their children participate in the demonstrations. Encourage the parents to ask questions and take part in the classroom as much as they have time to by coming in to share books and activities related to the books shared. Be sure to ask parents for their suggestions as to ways you can help.

If some of the parents cannot come, send home literature (in their first language, which you can prepare in advance with the help of other community members) with some ideas suggesting how they can encourage their child's personal reading in their home. Invite them to call you with questions and to visit the classroom another time that might be better for them.

20. Parents play an important role in enhancing their child's literacy and personal reading development. With your encouragement and initial planning, parents of your students can form book clubs and meet with other parents to discuss books. They can meet once a month or every other month, talk about the book they read, and

discuss which book to read for the next meeting. This would be a good way for parents to expand their own personal reading and serve as wonderful role models for developing their own families' personal reading. Moreover, many bookstores give discounts to book club members if they register their book club with the bookstore. Try it out! Get involved with your students' family literacy efforts. Perhaps some of the parents involved can later come into your classroom and share with the children the books they've read and the joy they are getting from their own personal reading.

Personal Reading: Appendix Grid

Type of Information Provided → Appendix Titles ↓	**A** Professional References and Resources for Locating Children's Literature	**B** Children's Literature Suggestions and Examples	**C** Feelings, Beliefs, Motivation, and Interest Inventories	**D** Parent, Family, and Community Connections
Professional Organizations	✓			
Published Lists of Children's Literature	✓			
Professional Books for Overview of Children's Literature	✓			
Professional Books to Support Classroom Reading	✓			
Nonfiction Trade Book Suggestions	✓			
Multicultural/Multiethnic Literature Suggestions	✓			
Literature to Help Children with Special Issues and Problems	✓			
Books for Read-Aloud Suggestions	✓			
Books that Suggest Picture Books and Predictable Books for Young Children	✓			
Magazine Suggestions for Children	✓			
Favorite Book Ideas	✓			
More Professional Resources	✓			
Sensitive Issues and Children's Problem Books		✓		
Children's Favorite Books		✓		
Uncovering Children's Feelings and Perceptions About Reading			✓	
Feelings, Beliefs, and Motivation Inventory			✓	
The Flippo Interest Inventory			✓	
The "Best Books" Inventory			✓	
My "Favorites" Inventory			✓	
Questions for Uncovering Motivations and Practical Needs			✓	
Activities for Uncovering Motivations and Practical Needs (Suggested for Younger Children)			✓	
Activities for Uncovering Motivations and Practical Needs (Suggested for Older Elementary Students)			✓	
Three-Way Conferencing: Sharing Personal Reading Information and Ideas				✓
How to Read a Book to Your Child				✓
Community Connections Think-About List				✓

Professional Organizations

Several professional organizations are actively involved in researching, promoting, listing, and providing information about children's literature. These are particularly recommended for their wealth and quality of available information. Their addresses follow:

American Library Association (ALA)
50 East Huron Street
Chicago, IL 60611

Office for Intellectual Freedom (OIF) at ALA
50 East Huron Street
Chicago, IL 60611

Children's Book Council (CBC)
12 West 37th Street, 2nd Floor
New York, NY 10018

International Reading Association (IRA)
800 Barksdale Road
PO Box 8139
Newark, DE 19714-8139

National Council of Teachers of English (NCTE)
1111 West Kenyon Road
Urbana, IL 61801-1096

Published Lists of Children's Literature

Many professional journals, other periodicals, and organizations regularly publish lists and recommendations of children's literature, including the previously cited ALA, CBC, IRA, and NCTE. In this section I provide specific information about these lists and
their sources. Many of these may be available for your reference in your school, public library or on the Internet.

Booklist is published by the American Library Association (ALA) once or twice each month. It contains listings of books
recommended for library purchase for both adults and children. Books that have been judged to be outstanding are noted with a
star. Bibliographies on selected topics are also included.

Book Links is also published by ALA. This magazine provides annotated bibliographies on many topics and themes for
teachers, librarians, bookstores, and others interested in children's literature, from preschool through eighth grade. Contact
Booklist or *Book Links* (see Appendix A–1, Professional Organizations, for the address).

The Horn Book magazine is published twice a month and reviews current children's books, classified by age level and subject.
It also provides articles on Caldecott and Newbery Medal winners, reviews books in Spanish, reviews books that have recently
been republished in paperback, and provides a list of "outstanding books" each year. Contact *The Horn Book*, 14 Beacon Street,
Boston, MA 02108-9765.

Journal of Children's Literature is published twice a year by the Children's Literature Assembly, an affiliate of NCTE. Each fall
issue contains that year's list of notable children's trade books. Contact the NCTE (see Appendix A–1, Professional Organizations,
for the address).

The Language Arts, a journal published by NCTE, publishes a list of notable children's books, yearly, in its October issue.
Contact the NCTE.

Multicultural Review reviews books for children and young adults and also reviews other multicultural materials in each of its
quarterly issues. Contact *Multicultural Review*, Greenwood Publishing Group, 88 Post Road West, Box 5007, Westport, CT 06881-5007.

The New York Times Book Review devotes a fall and a spring Book Reviews section to children's books. Also, in November and
December, it publishes selected lists of outstanding children's books. Contact *The New York Times Book Review*, 229 West 43rd
Street, New York, NY 10036.

The Reading Teacher, a journal published by IRA, publishes "Children's Choices" each year in its October issue. This annual
bibliography is a list of books (compiled by the IRA and the Children's Book Council, CBC) chosen by children as their very favorites.
Contact the IRA or the CBC (see Appendix A–1, Professional Organizations, for the addresses).

Each November, *The Reading Teacher* also publishes the Teachers' Choices list. Teachers' Choices is a list of books chosen by
teachers as outstanding for curriculum use. Contact the IRA for the Teachers' Choices list.

The School Library Journal is published monthly, reviewing new books for children and young adults. The reviews are categorized by four age levels and under fiction and nonfiction designations. Outstanding books are rated with a star and are included in
the Best Book list published in each December's issue. Children's books in Spanish are also reviewed. Contact *The School Library
Journal*, PO Box 1978, Marion, OH 43306-2078.

Professional Books for Overviews of Children's Literature

Many professional books are available to the classroom teacher looking for information about and ideas for good children's literature. In this section and the others that follow in these appendixes, I've cited some of these sources, organizing them into categories that describe their use.

The overviews of children's literature books generally provide discussions of children's literature and suggestions for children's literature in a wide variety of genres. Many of these books also include samples of children's literature, lists of award-winning books, suggested magazines for children, addresses of publishers of children's books, CD-ROM databases of children's books, and other valuable resources relating to children's literature. The full citations for each of these can be found in the references at the end of this book. Many of these professional resources may be available in your college or public library. Always ask for the most recent edition of each.

Galda and Cullinan (2006), *Literature and the Child*

Glazer and Giorgis (2005), *Literature for Young Children*

Hancock (2004), *A Celebration of Literature and Response*

Huck, Kiefer, Hepler, and Hickman (2004), *Children's Literature in the Elementary School*

Jacobs and Tunnell (2004), *Children's Literature, Briefly*

Lukens (2003), *A Critical Handbook of Children's Literature*

Norton and Norton (2003), *Through the Eyes of a Child: An Introduction to Children's Literature*

Russell (2005), *Literature for Children: A Short Introduction*

Stoodt-Hill and Amspaugh-Corson (2005), *Children's Literature: Discovery for a Lifetime*

Sutherland (1997), *Children and Books*

Professional Books to Support Classroom Reading

While the books and resources listed in this Appendix provide help and support for developing personal reading, the following books seem particularly appropriate for ideas and suggestions that would facilitate reading, discussion of reading, and a literate environment in the early childhood and elementary classroom.

Cullinan (1992), *Invitation to Read: More Children's Literature in the Reading Program*

Cullinan (1993a), *Children's Voices: Talk in the Classroom*

Day, Spiegel, McLellan, and Brown (2002), *Moving Forward with Literature Circles*

Hill, Noe, and Johnson (2001), *Literature Circles Resource Guide*

Paratore and McCormack (1997), *Peer Talk in the Classroom: Learning from Research*

Roser and Martinez, eds. (1995), *Book Talk and Beyond: Children and Teachers Respond to Literature*

Slaughter (1993), *Beyond Storybooks: Young Children and the Shared Book Experience*

Nonfiction Trade Book Suggestions

These books contain many suggested ideas for using more nonfiction trade books in your classroom curriculum.

Bamford and Kristo (2003), *Making Facts Come Alive: Choosing and Using Nonfiction Literature K–8*

Cullinan (1993b), *Fact and Fiction: Literature Across the Curriculum*

Freeman and Person (1998), *Connecting Informational Children's Books with Content Area Learning*

Freeman and Person, eds. (1992), *Using Nonfiction Trade Books in the Elementary Classroom: From Ants to Zeppelins*

Kletzien and Dreher (2004), *Informational Text in K–3 Classrooms: Helping Children Read and Write*

Kristo and Bamford (2004), *Nonfiction in Focus*

Multicultural/Multiethnic Literature Suggestions

These books contain many good ideas for using multicultural literature in your classroom, as well as suggestions for specific children's literature for a variety of diverse cultures and ethnicities.

Hansen-Krening, Aoki, and Mizokawa (2003), *Kaleidoscope: A Multicultural Booklet for Grades K–8*

Harris (1997), *Using Multiethnic Literature in the Grades K–8 Classroom*

Hayden (1992), *Venture into Cultures: A Resource Book of Multicultural Materials and Programs*

Miller-Lachmann (1995), *Global Voices, Global Visions: A Core Collection of Multicultural Books*

Miller-Lachmann (1992), *Our Family, Our Friends, Our World: An Annotated Guide to Significant Multicultural Books for Children and Teenagers*

Norton (2005), *Multicultural Children's Literature: Through the Eyes of Many Children*

Schon and Berkin (1996), *Introducción a la Literatura Infantil y Juvenil*

Young, ed. (2004), *Happily Ever After: Sharing Folk Literature with Elementary and Middle School Students*

Zarrillo (1994), *Multicultural Literature, Multicultural Teaching: Units for the Elementary Grades.*

Many of the books listed in Appendix A–3 also include multicultural/multiethnic literature suggestions.

Literature to Help Children with Special Issues and Problems

These books provide literature suggestions for children in a wide variety of special areas of concern, including divorce, death, adoption, foster care, family configurations, siblings, aging, abuse, sexuality, special needs, separation and loss, drug and substance abuse, moving, and various disabilities. Not all of these issues are dealt with in any one of these books; however, their titles will give you a fairly good idea of their coverage.

Friedberg, Mullins, and Sukiennik (1992), *Portraying Persons with Disabilities: An Annotated Bibliography of Nonfiction for Children and Teenagers*

Rasinski and Gillespie (1992), *Sensitive Issues: An Annotated Guide to Children's Literature K–6*

Robertson (1992), *Portraying Persons with Disabilities: An Annotated Bibliography of Fiction for Children and Teenagers*

Rudman (1995), *Children's Literature: An Issues Approach*

Rudman, Gagne, and Bernstein (1994), *Books to Help Children Cope with Separation and Loss*

Several of the books listed in Appendix A–3 also include some literature suggestions for some special issues, problems, and disabilities with which children may have to deal.

Books for Read-Aloud Suggestions

These books provide a discussion of ideas and activities for follow-ups to read-alouds. Additionally, good books and stories to read aloud to young children as well as to older children are suggested.

Campbell (2001), *Read-Alouds with Young Children*

Trelease (1992), *Hey! Listen to This: Stories to Read Aloud*

Trelease (2001), *The Read-Aloud Handbook*

Many of the books listed in Appendix A–3 also include read-aloud book suggestions.

Books That Suggest Picture Books and Predictable Books for Young Children

These books suggest ideas and literature that are particularly relevant to the needs of the teacher of young children. They suggest picture books and predictable books, use of them in the classroom, and many teaching ideas.

Beaty (1994), *Picture Book Storytelling: Literature Activities for Young Children*

Cianciolo (1997), *Picture Books for Children*

Slaughter (1993), *Beyond Storybooks: Young Children and the Shared Book Experience*

Additionally, many of the books in Appendix A–3 include picture books and predictable books.

Magazine Suggestions for Children

This provides a resource for information regarding available magazines and other periodicals for children.

Stoll (1997), *Magazines for Kids and Teens*

Additionally, some of the books listed under other categories of professional books in these appendixes make suggestions regarding children's magazines and newspapers.

Favorite Book Ideas

These books provide listings of children's favorite books to read, and teachers' favorite books to use in the curriculum. Additionally, many wonderful suggestions for classroom follow-up activities with these books are shared.

IRA (1994), *Teachers' Favorite Books for Kids*

IRA and CBC (1992), *Kids' Favorite Books: Children's Choices 1989–1991*

IRA and CBC (1995), *More Kids' Favorite Books*

Post, Scott, and Theberge (2000), *Celebrating Children's Choices: 25 Years of Children's Favorite Books*

More Professional Resources

Many of the books already suggested in other categories provide research sources for teachers, and all of the books listed in all categories are excellent professional resources. However, the following books provide listings of almost all the resources related to children's literature that anyone might need. They provide an excellent starting place for the teacher or other educators who want to quickly see a range of what is available.

Short (1995), *Research & Professional Resources in Children's Literature: Piecing a Patchwork Quilt*

Sullivan (2004), *The Children's Literature Lover's Book of Lists*

Sensitive Issues and Children's Problems Books

In this list, I pull from the recommendations of Rudman (1995) and others to provide a few examples of books in a variety of sensitive and/or problem areas.

Adoption

Lifton, B. J. 1993. *Tell Me a Real Adoption Story*. New York: Alfred A. Knopf.

Rivera, G. 1976. *A Special Kind of Courage: Profiles of Young Americans*. New York: Simon & Schuster.

Wasson, V. 1977. *The Chosen Baby*, 3rd rev. ed. Philadelphia: J. B. Lippincott.

Aging

Ackerman, K. 1990. *Just Like Max*. New York: Alfred A. Knopf.

Hickman, M. W. 1985. *When James Allen Whitaker's Grandfather Came to Stay*. Nashville, TN: Abingdon.

Leiner, K. 1987. *Between Old Friends*. New York: Franklin Watts.

Moore, E. 1988. *Grandma's Promise*. New York: Lothrop, Lee & Shepard.

Child Abuse

Anderson, M. Q. 1978. *Step on a Crack*. New York: Atheneum.

Hunt, I. 1976. *The Lottery Rose*. New York: Charles Scribner's Sons.

Lowery, L. 1994. *Laurie Tells*. Minneapolis, MN: Carolrhoda Books.

Roberts, W. D. 1978. *Don't Hurt Laurie!* New York: Atheneum.

Death

Anders, R. 1978. *A Look at Death*. Minneapolis, MN: Larner.

Burch, R. 1970. *Simon and the Game of Chance*. New York: Viking.

dePaola, T. 1973. *Nana Upstairs & Nana Downstairs*. New York: G. P. Putnam's Sons.

Mellonie, B. 1983. *Lifetimes: The Beautiful Way to Explain Death to Children*. New York: Bantam Books.

Disabilities

Baldwin, A. M. 1978. *A Little Time*. New York: Viking.

O'Shaughnessy, E. 1992. *Somebody Called Me Retarded Today . . . and My Heart Felt Sad*. New York: Walker and Company.

Peusner, S. 1977. *Keep Stompin' Till the Music Stops*. New York: Seabury Press.

Wolf, B. 1974. *Don't Feel Sorry for Paul*. Philadelphia: J. B. Lippincott.

Divorce

Blume, J. 1972. *It's Not the End of the World*. New York: Bantam Press.

Krementz, J. 1988. *How It Feels When Parents Divorce*. New York: Alfred A. Knopf.

Mann, P. 1978. *My Father Lives in a Downtown Hotel*. New York: Doubleday.

(Continues)

Families: Single Parent

Gilbert, S. 1982. *How to Live with a Single Parent*. New York: Lothrop, Lee & Shepard.

Gould, D. 1988. *Brendan's Best-Timed Birthday*. New York: Bradbury.

Johnson, D. 1990. *What Will Mommy Do When I'm at School?* New York: Macmillan.

Families: Stepparents and Stepfamilies

Boyd, L. 1987. *The Not-So-Wicked Stepmother*. New York: Viking.

MacLachlan, P. 1985. *Sarah, Plain and Tall*. New York: Harper.

Nixon, J. L. 1985. *Maggie Too*. San Diego: Harcourt Brace Jovanovich.

Park, B. 1989. *My Mother Got Married (and Other Disasters)*. New York: Alfred A. Knopf.

Sobol, H. L. 1979. *My Other-Mother, My Other-Father*. New York: Macmillan.

Families: Extended

MacLachlan, P. 1991. *Journey*. New York: Delacorte.

Shasha, M. 1992. *Night of the Moonjellies*. New York: Simon & Schuster.

Snyder, Z. K. 1990. *Libby on Wednesday*. New York: Delacorte.

Whelan, G. 1992. *Bringing the Farmhouse Home*. New York: Simon & Schuster.

Williams, V. B. 1982. *A Chair for My Mother*. New York: Greenwillow.

Fear

Berkey, B., and V. Berkey 1978. *Robbers, Bones, and Mean Dogs*. Reading, MA: Addison-Wesley.

Clyne, P. E. 1977. *Tunnels of Terror*. Boston: Atlantic Monthly Press.

Mayer, M. 1991. *You're the Scaredy-Cat*. Roxbury, CT: Rainbird Press.

McCloskey, R. 1952. *One Morning in Maine*. New York: Viking.

Gender Roles

Gauch, P. L. 1971. *Christina Katerina & the Box*. New York: Coward-McCann.

Hilton, N. 1990. *The Long Red Scarf*. Minneapolis, MN: Carolrhoda Books.

Isadora, R. 1980. *My Ballet Class*. New York: Greenwillow.

MacLachlan, P. 1979. *The Sick Day*. New York: Pantheon.

McPherson, S. S. 1992. *I Speak for the Women: A Story About Lucy Stone*. Minneapolis, MN: Carolrhoda.

Heritage

Allison, D. W. 1992. *This Is the Key to the Kingdom*. Boston: Little, Brown.

Ancona, G. 1993. *Powwow*. San Diego: Harcourt Brace Jovanovich.

Bang, M. 1985. *The Paper Crane*. New York: Greenwillow.

Bryan, A. 1989. *Turtle Knows Your Name*. New York: Atheneum.

Hurwitz, J. 1980. *Once I Was a Plum Tree*. New York: Morrow.

Lawrence, J. 1993. *The Great Migration*. New York: Harper.

Hospitalization

Howe, J. 1994. *The Hospital Book*. New York: Morrow.

Rey, M. and H. A. Rey. 1966. *Curious George Goes to the Hospital*. Boston: Houghton Mifflin.

Sobol, H. L. 1975. *Jeff's Hospital Book*. New York: Henry Z. Walck.

Love

Graham, J. 1976. *I Love You, Mouse*. San Diego, CA: Harcourt Brace Jovanovich.

Sonneborn, R. 1970. *Friday Night Is Papa Night*. New York: Viking.

Viscardi, H. 1975. *The Phoenix Child: A Story of Love*. Middlebury, VT: Paul S. Eriksson.

Self-Awareness

Ardizzone, E. 1970. *The Wrong Side of the Bed*. New York: Doubleday.

Carlson, N. 1988. *I Like Me*. New York: Viking.

Hooks, W. H. 1977. *Doug Meets the Nutcracker*. New York: Frederick Warne.

Lee, H. A. 1978. *Seven Feet Four and Growing*. Philadelphia: Westminster.

Sibling Rivalry

Alexander, M. G. 1975. *I'll Be the Horse If You'll Play with Me*. New York: Dial.

Dragonwagon, C. 1983. *I Hate My Brother Harry*. New York: Harper.

Hazen, B. S. 1979. *If It Weren't for Benjamin*. New York: Human Science Press.

Lexau, J. M. 1972. *Emily and the Klunky Baby and the Next Door Dog*. New York: Dial.

Zolotow, C. 1966. *If It Weren't for You*. New York: Harper & Row.

Twins

Aliki. 1986. *Jack and Jake*. New York: Greenwillow.

Cleary, B. 1967. *Mitch and Amy*. New York: Morrow.

Fair, S. 1982. *The Bedspread*. New York: Morrow.

Children's Favorite Books

Children like books for various valid reasons. In one study, conducted by Wilson and Abrahamson (1988), fifth-grade students were asked about their favorite classic books. They rated and ranked the following classics as their favorites: *Charlotte's Web*; *Little House in the Big Woods*; *The Secret Garden*; *The Hobbit*; *The Lion, the Witch, and the Wardrobe*; *Heidi*; *The Borrowers*; and *The Moffats*. When asked why *Charlotte's Web* was their highest-ranked book, they indicated because (1) it was a fantasy but it was made to seem very real; (2) it was personal and it evoked an emotional response from them; (3) they loved the animal characters; and (4) they liked the author's style.

In the listings that follow, you will find a selection of book titles for various age groups that literally hundreds of children in those age groups have read, voted for, and selected as their favorites. These titles were taken from many years of "Children's Choices" compiled and published by IRA and CBC. For full listings of each year's favorite children's books, consult the October issues of *The Reading Teacher*.

These lists are designed not only for use by teachers, but they can be used by parents, grandparents, and others who want to encourage children's personal reading. It also should be noted that books listed on the beginning readers' list can also be enjoyed by much younger children as well as more advanced readers, and many books for more advanced readers would be enjoyable for younger children if read aloud by teachers or family.

For Beginning Readers (Ages Five to Six)

Big Pumpkin (1992) by E. Silverman. New York: Macmillan.

Bill and Pete to the Rescue (1998) by T. dePaola. New York: Putnam.

Bus-a-Saurus Bop (2003) by D. Z. Shore. New York: Bloomsbury USA Children's Books.

Captain Bob Sets Sail (2000) by R. Schotter. New York: Atheneum.

Clifford the Firehouse Dog (1994) by N. Bridwell. New York: Scholastic.

Cock-a-Moo-Moo (2002) by J. Dallas-Conté. Boston: Little, Brown.

Copy Cat (1997) by J. Mole. Las Vegas, NV: Kingfisher Books.

Draw Me a Star (1992) by E. Carle. New York: Philomel.

Easy to See Why (1993) by F. Gwynne. New York: Simon & Schuster.

Five Little Monkeys Sitting in a Tree (1991) by E. Christelow. New York: Clarion.

Flip and Flop (2001) by D. Apperley. New York: Orchard.

The Giant Zucchini (1993) by C. Siracusa. New York: Hyperion.

The Great Snake Escape (1994) by M. Coxe. New York: HarperCollins.

How Do You Say It Today, Jesse Bear? (1992) by N. W. Carlstrom. New York: Macmillan.

Hunter's Best Friend at School (2002) by L. M. Elliot. New York: HarperCollins.

Ice Cream Larry (1999) by D. Pinkwater. Tarrytown, NY: Marshall Cavendish.

King Kenrick's Splinter (1994) by S. Derby. New York: Walker.

Matthew's Dream (1991) by L. Lionni. New York: Alfred A. Knopf.

Max's Wacky Taxi Day (1997) by M. Grover. San Diego, CA: Harcourt Brace.

Monkey Soup (1992) by L. Sachar. New York: Alfred A. Knopf.

Mouse in Love (2000) by R. Kraus. New York: Orchard.

The Mouse Who Ate Bananas (2001) by K. Faulkner. New York: Orchard.

The Old Dog (1995) by J. Ransome. New York: HarperCollins.

Sheep in a Shop (1991) by N. Shaw. Boston: Houghton Mifflin.

Snow Ponies (2001) by C. Cotten. New York: Henry Holt.

Tangle Town (1997) by K. Cyrus. New York: Farrar, Straus and Giroux.

Ten Tiny Turtles: A Crazy Counting Book (1995) by P. Cherrill. Boston: Houghton Mifflin.

Trade-in Mother (1993) by M. Russo. New York: Greenwillow.

What Dads Can't Do (2000) by D. Wood. New York: Simon & Schuster.

When I Was Five (1996) by A. Howard. San Diego, CA: Harcourt Brace.

When I Was Little: A Four-Year-Old's Memoir of Her Youth (1993) by J. L. Curtis. New York: HarperCollins.

The Winter Duckling (1990) by K. Polette. St. Louis, MO: Milliken.

For Young Readers (Ages Six to Eight)

An Alligator Named . . . Alligator (1991) by L. G. Grambling. Hauppauge, NY: Barron's.

Andrew's Amazing Monsters (1993) by K. H. Berlan. New York: Atheneum.

Arthur's Family Vacation (1993) by M. Brown. Boston: Little, Brown.

A Trip to Dinosaur Time (2002) by M. Foreman. Cambridge, MA: Candlewick Press.

Bats Around the Clock (2000) by K. Appelt. New York: HarperCollins.

Benjamin Bigfoot (1993) by M. Serfozo. New York: McElderry Books.

The Big Bug Ball (1999) by D. Lillegard. New York: Putnam.

A Box Can Be Many Things (1997) by D. M. Rau. Danbury, CT: Children's Press/Grolier.

The Boxer and the Princess (1998) by H. Heine. New York: Simon & Schuster.

Captain Abolul's Pirate School (1994) by C. McNaughton. Cambridge, MA: Candlewick Press.

Cleo and the Coyote (1996) by E. Levy. New York: HarperCollins.

Courtney (1994) by J. Burningham. New York: Crown.

Dogs Don't Wear Sneakers (1993) by L. Numeroff. New York: Simon & Schuster.

Don't Wake Up Mama! Another Five Little Monkeys Story (1992) by E. Christelow. New York: Clarion.

Dragon's Fat Cat (1992) by D. Pilkey. New York: Orchard.

Dragon Soup (1996) by A. Williams. Tiburon, CA: H. J. Kramar/Starseed.

Earthquake in the Third Grade (1993) by L. Myers. New York: Clarion.

Emergency (2002) by M. Mayo. Minneapolis, MN: Lerner.

Giraffes Can't Dance (2001) by G. Andreae. New York: Orchard.

The Halloween House (1997) by E. Silverman. New York: Farrar, Straus & Giroux.

Hamburger Heaven (1999) by W. H. Lee. Boston: Houghton Mifflin.

John Willy and Freddy McGee (1998) by H. Meade. Mahwah, NJ: Troll.

Miss Spider's Tea Party (1994) by D. Kirk. New York: Scholastic.

Mona the Vampire (1991) by S. Holleyman. New York: Delacorte.

Mrs. Katz and Tush (1992) by P. Polacco. New York: Dell.

Mucky Moose (1991) by J. Allen. New York: Macmillan.

My Cats Nick and Nora (1995) by B. Moser. New York: Blue Sky Press.

My Life With the Wave (1997) by C. Cowan. New York: Lothrop, Lee & Shepard.

The Night I Followed the Dog (1994) by N. Laden. San Francisco: Chronicle Books.

The Night Iguana Left Home (1999) by M. McDonald. New York: DK Ink.

Pete's a Pizza (1998) by W. Steig. New York: diCapua/HarperCollins.

The Practically Perfect Pajamas (2000) by E. Brooks. New York: Winslow Press.

Trick-or-Treat on Milton Street (2001) by L. Bullard. Minneapolis, MN: Lerner.

A Trip to Dinosaur Time (2002) by M. Foreman. Cambridge, MA: Candlewick Press.

Wagons West! (1996) by R. Gerrard. New York: Farrar, Straus & Giroux.

Without Words (1995) by J. Ryder. Boston: Sierra Club Books for Children.

For Intermediate Readers (Ages Eight to Ten)

Alice in April (1993) by P. R. Naylor. New York: Atheneum.

A to Z Mysteries: The Haunted Hotel (1999) by R. Roy. New York: Random House.

Best Enemies Again (1991) by K. Leverich. New York: Greenwillow.

Best Friends (1993) by E. Reuter. Cedarhurst, NY: Yellow Brick Road/Pitspopany Press.

Doesn't Fall Off His Horse (1994) by V. A. Stroud. New York: Dial.

Dracula's Tomb (1998) by C. McNaughton. Cambridge, MA: Candlewick Press.

Fly High! The Story of Bessie Coleman (2001) by L. Borden and M. K. Kroeger. New York: Margaret K. McElderry Books/Simon & Schuster.

Fourth Grade Rats (1991) by J. Spinelli. New York: Scholastic.

The Ghost of Popcorn Hill (1993) by B. R. Wright. New York: Holiday House.

Grady's in the Silo (2003) by U. B. Townsend. Gretna, LA: Pelican.

The Hamster of the Baskervilles (2002) by B. Hale. San Diego, CA: Harcourt.

The High Rise Glorious Skittle Skat Roarious Sky Pie Angel Food Cake (1990) by N. Willard. San Diego, CA: Harcourt Brace.

Hoops (1997) by R. Burleigh. San Diego, CA: Harcourt Brace.

Humpty Dumpty Egg-Splodes (2001) by K. O'Malley. New York: Walker.

Jesse Owens: Olympic Star (1992) by P. McKissack and F. McKissack. Hillside, NJ: Enslow.

The Last Princess: The Story of Princess Ka'iulani of Hawai'i (1991) by F. Stanley. New York: Four Winds.

The Legend of the Loon (2000) by K. Wargin. Chelsea, MI: Sleeping Bear Press.

The Librarian Who Measured the Earth (1994) by K. Lasky. Boston: Little, Brown.

Meet Addy (1993) by C. Porter. Middleton, WI: Pleasant Company.

Mercedes and the Chocolate Pilot: A True Story of the Berlin Airlift and the Candy That Dropped from the Sky (2002) by M. T. Raven. Chelsea, MI: Sleeping Bear Press.

Muggie Maggie (1991) by B. Cleary. New York: William Morrow.

Oh Boy, Amelia! (2001) by M. Moss. Middleton, WI: Pleasant.

Paul Revere's Ride: The Landlord's Tale (2003) by H. W. Longfellow. New York: HarperCollins.

Rattlesnack Dance: True Tales, Mysteries, and Rattlesnack Ceremonies (1997) by J. O. Dewey. Honesdale, PA: Boyd Mills Press.

The River (1991) by G. Paulsen. New York: Delacorte.

The Sea of Tranquility (1996) by M. Haddon. San Diego, CA: Harcourt Brace.

She's Wearing a Dead Bird on Her Head (1995) by D. Catrow. New York: Hyperion.

Skeleton Man (2001) by J. Bruchac. New York: HarperCollins.

The Spider and the Fly (2002) by M. Howitt. New York: Simon & Schuster.

Storm (1993) by J. Wood. New York: Thomson Learning.

(Continues)

Three Magic Balls (2000) by R. Egielski. New York: Laura Geringer Books/HarperCollins.

Thunder Rose (2003) by J. Nolen. San Diego, CA: Silver Whistle/Harcourt Children's Books.

Who's in the Hall? A Mystery in Four Chapters (2000) by B. Hearne. New York: Greenwillow.

The Wretched Stone (1991) by C. Van Allsburg. Boston: Houghton Mifflin.

For Advanced Readers (Ages Ten to Thirteen)

Act I, Act II, Act Normal (2003) by M. Weston. New York: Roaring Brook Press.

Alone in the House (1991) by E. Plante. New York: Avon.

Becoming Joe DiMaggio (2002) by M. Testa. Cambridge, MA: Candlewick Press.

Beyond the Mango Tree (1998) by A. B. Zemser. New York: Greenwillow.

Blue Sky, Butterfly (1996) by J. V. Leeuwen. New York: Dial.

Crash (1996) by J. Spinelli. New York: Alfred A. Knopf.

Crosstown (1993) by K. Makris. New York: Avon.

Dogs Don't Tell Jokes (1991) by L. Sachar. New York: Alfred A. Knopf.

Don't Tell Anyone (2000) by P. Kehret. New York: Dutton Children's Books.

The Face on the Milk Carton (1990) by C. B. Cooney. New York: Bantam Books.

Finding Buck McHenry (1991) by A. Slote. New York: HarperCollins.

Flip-Flop Girl (1994) by K. Paterson. New York: Lodestar Books.

Ghost Brother (1990) by C. S. Adler. New York: Clarion Books.

Ghost Stories (1993) Compiled by R. Westall. Las Vegas, NV: Kingfisher Books.

The Giver (1993) by L. Lowry. Boston: Houghton Mifflin.

Into the Candlelit Room and Other Strange Tales (1999) by T. McKean. New York: Putnam.

L. Frank Baum: Royal Historian of Oz (1992) by A. S. Carpenter and J. Shirley. Minneapolis, MN: Lerner.

Letting Swift River Go (1992) by J. Yolen. Boston: Little, Brown.

Magic Can Be Murder (2000) by V. V. Velde. San Diego, CA: Harcourt Children's Books.

Mama, Let's Dance (1991) by P. Hermes. Boston: Little, Brown.

A Million Visions of Peace: Wisdom from the Friends of Old Turtle (1995) by J. Garrison and A. Tubesing. Duluth, MN: Pfeifer-Hamilton.

Nightjohn (1993) by G. Paulsen. New York: Delacorte/Bantam Doubleday Dell.

PredicKtions (2003) by J. Halliday. New York: Margaret K. McElderry Books/Simon & Schuster Children's.

Rosa Parks: My Story (1990) by R. Parks with J. Haskins. New York: Dial.

Skin Deep and Other Teenage Reflections (1995) by A. S. Medearis. New York: Atheneum.

Snowboarding (1997) by L. D. Brimner. Danbury, CT: Franklin Watts.

Watchers #4: War (1999) by P. Lerangis. New York: Apple/Scholastic.

What Daddy Did (1991) by N. Shusterman. Boston: Little, Brown.

Where I'd Like to Be (2003) by F. O. Dowell. New York: Atheneum/Simon & Schuster Children's.

The Wish (2000) by G. C. Levine. New York: HarperCollins.

Finally, did you know that there are well over one hundred different awards given each year for children's books? These awards include the Newbery Medal, Caldecott Medal, Boston Globe–Horn Book Awards, IRA Children's Book Award, and many others. Each one of these awards uses its own selection process with some selected by children, some by adults, and some by international and/or local or regional groups. A comprehensive listing of the various award winners can be found in *Children's Books: Awards and Prizes*, updated and published periodically by the Children's Book Council (e.g., see the 1996 publication cited in the references of this book). The latest publication of this material should be available in your school or public library for your use and reference. Additionally, the most current books of children's literature can be consulted—most of them contain information on these awards as well. (See the books listed in Appendix A–3.)

Uncovering Children's Feelings and Perceptions About Reading

1. If you were asked to describe yourself as a reader, what would you say?

_____
_____
_____
_____
_____ .

2. What do you think your last year's teacher thought about you as a reader? Why?

_____
_____
_____
_____
_____ .

3. How do you feel when you read? Do you feel good? Do you feel bad? Why?

_____
_____
_____
_____
_____ .

4. What do you think your parents and family think about your reading? Do they think you are a good reader? Do they think you are a bad reader? Who thinks these things? Why?

_____
_____
_____
_____
_____ .

5. Who is a good reader that you know? What makes him or her a good reader?

_____
_____
_____
_____
_____ .

Feelings, Beliefs, and Motivation Inventory

1. I like to read most when I _____

   _____

   _____

   _____ .

2. When I read, I feel _____

   _____

   _____

   _____ .

3. I would read more if _____

   _____

   _____

   _____ .

4. I read better than _____ but not as good as _____ .

   I could be just as good if _____

   _____

   _____

   _____ .

5. Here is a picture of me reading:

   I feel _____

   _____

   _____ .

The Flippo Interest Inventory

Directions: This inventory can be given orally to both younger and older students, or you can have your older students complete it independently. To obtain accurate and complete information, it is recommended that you record students' oral responses exactly as they give them to you. If students ask for assistance with their written responses, feel free to help them.

1. What are the things (topics) you like most to read about? Why?

2. What are the things you like most to do? Why?

3. Are there some new things (topics) that you are interested in learning about? Why?

4. What would you like to do when you grow up? Why? List or tell everything you can think of that you would really like to do.

5. What kinds of things do you like to read about—or watch TV, videos, or movies about—just for fun or excitement? Why?

6. Have you heard or read about anything new or unusual (in school or at home) that you would like to learn more about? Why?

7. Do you like to do things by following directions such as cooking, building or assembling, sewing, or writing away for things? Which do you like? Why?

8. What is your favorite kind of music?

9. Do you have any special hobbies? What are they? Why are they especially interesting?

10. Do you have any favorite sports? What are they?

11. Do you have any pets? What kinds?

12. Are you interested in any role-playing games? If so, which ones? (Note: You may want to reword these questions for use with younger students.)

13. Do you have some special concerns or problems that you would like to explore, work on, or change? If so, would you like some help finding resources or information? (Indicate to students that they do not have to answer these questions, but if they do, their answers will be confidential. Also note that you will need to reword these questions for use with younger students.)

14. If you could do anything in the world and money was no object, what would you like to do? Why?

15. If you could go anywhere in the world and money and time were not problems, where would you like to go? Why?

16. What are the names (titles) of your favorite books? Who are your favorite authors?

17. Of all the books and authors listed in item 16, which/who is absolutely your favorite book and favorite author? Why?

18. If you wanted to tell people about this book (and/or author), and convince them to read it (or read other books by the author), what would you say?

19. If some people wanted to give you a number of books, magazines, or other types of printed materials to read, what kind should they give you? Why? Can you name some particular titles?

20. If a writer told you she would write a book, just for you, about anything, but she needed to know what you would want in the book, what would you say?

Appendix C–4

The "Best Books" Inventory

1. The names of the books I like best are _____

_____

_____

_____

_____

_____

_____

_____ .

2. They are about _____

_____

_____

_____

_____

_____

_____

_____ .

3. They are really good because _____

_____

_____

_____

_____

_____

_____ .

4. I would like to read more books about_____

_____

_____

_____

_____

_____

_____ .

My "Favorites" Inventory

Directions: The teacher of early-grade children would read the following statement to the children.

Statement: "Lots of people are happiest when they're doing their favorite things. Please draw a picture of yourself doing your favorite things. Let's call it 'favorite things'. "

   When each child is finished with his picture, the teacher circulates around the classroom and asks each child to tell what favorite things are in the picture. Using sentence strips, the teacher writes the favorite things and attaches the listing to each child's picture. Children are encouraged to hang their pictures with the listings up for display and tell the other youngsters about their favorite things.

Questions for Uncovering Motivations and Practical Needs

1. Is there something special that you would like to learn how do do?

2. Is there something special that you would like to get more information about, or that you have to do?

3. Is there something special that you would like to share with the class?

4. Is there something special that the teacher can help you with?

5. Is there something special that someone else in our class, or in our school, can help you with? Who?

6. When you don't come to school, what kind of things do you like to do?

7. When you don't come to school, what kind of things do you have to do?

8. Who do you do these things with?

9. Who would you like to do these things with?

10. If you could wish for three things, what would you wish for?

Activities for Uncovering Motivations and Practical Needs (Suggested for Younger Children)

1. Draw a picture of something you like to do.

2. Draw a picture of somebody you like to do it with. Who is it?

3. Draw a picture of something you would like to do, but don't know how to do it.

4. Draw a picture of somebody you would like to do it with.

5. Draw a picture of your whole family. Who is in the picture? Who do you like to do things with? What kind of things do you do?

Activities for Uncovering Motivations and Practical Needs (Suggested for Older Elementary Students)

Directions for the teacher: Older students could also draw or write their answers to these questions if they prefer not to pantomime.

1. Do you know how to do a pantomime? Pantomime is acting without words. Can you pantomime something you *like to do*, and we will try to guess what it is?

2. Can you pantomime something that you would like to *learn how to do*, and we will try to guess what it is?

3. Can you pantomime someone you like to, or would like to, do these things with? We will try to guess who it is.

4. If you could have three wishes to *change* anything, what would you change? Pantomime, and we will try to guess your wishes.

5. If you could have three wishes to *have* anything, what would you like to have? Pantomime, and we will try to guess your wishes.

Three-Way Conferencing: Sharing Personal Reading Information and Ideas

Date	Child's first and last name	Grade
My thoughts regarding the accomplishments of our sharing	My/our thoughts regarding the accomplishments of our sharing	My thoughts regarding the accomplishments of our sharing
[Child's name]	[Family member's name(s)]	[Teacher's name]

Plans for personal reading:

_____

_____

_____

_____

_____

_____

_____

How to Read a Book to Your Child

Reading a book to your child should be a pleasant experience for both of you, a time you and your child can relish together. Use the following list of steps only as a guide to help you and your child develop your own unique way of sharing books.

1. Carefully select a book for your child from a selection of good children's books. Or select several books and let the child choose one from the group. Or allow your child to independently select a book. (It is probably best to alternate your methods of selecting a book to be read from the three ways suggested, but when your child *wants* you to read a particular book, please honor her request.)

2. Talk about the book before you begin to read it so that your youngster knows the title, is familiar with the cover, and has been told the author's name. This will allow the child to anticipate the book. This will also help the child realize that someone wrote the book and that a book is someone else's thoughts, ideas, and talk written down.

3. Read the book to your child, stopping often to point at or talk about different things in the pictures, according to the child's interests. (But remember, throughout the reading, you are *not teaching* the book, you want this experience to be relaxing and very pleasurable for your child.)

4. As you read the book, ask questions that your child can answer by looking for clues in the pictures or making inferences from what has already been read. Allow your child time to answer, and praise your child's comments whenever possible. If you disagree with the answer, ask your youngster about it. If the answer is not at all applicable, talk about other possible answers to the same question. Be careful not to say, "That's wrong," "You didn't understand," or "No, that's not right."

5. After you have read the book, talk about things in the book with which your child is familiar, or things in which the child is interested. Encourage your youngster to talk about the book.

6. Occasionally, allow your child an opportunity to illustrate a favorite part of the book after you have finished reading it. Sometimes let the child verbalize the theme of the book to you as you write down the child's exact words; then display them with the picture.

7. Very often your child will want to read a favorite book to you. Allow this whenever possible. *Do not correct* errors. The child is not reading words but is retelling the story from memory. This gives you a chance to observe the progress of your child's oral language and memory development. This practice and opportunity will be very good, providing that you are supportive and don't turn this into a reading lesson.

Community Connections Think-About List

Connections to make	Resources for our students	Resources we can offer
_____	_____	_____
_____	_____	_____
_____	_____	_____
_____	_____	_____
_____	_____	_____
_____	_____	_____
_____	_____	_____
_____	_____	_____
_____	_____	_____
_____	_____	_____
_____	_____	_____
_____	_____	_____
_____	_____	_____
_____	_____	_____
_____	_____	_____

References

Allington, R. L. 1994. "The Schools We Have. The Schools We Need." *The Reading Teacher* 48: 14–29.

Alvermann, D. E., and J. T. Guthrie. 1993. "Themes and Directions of the National Reading Research Center." *Perspectives in Reading Research* 1: 1–11.

Anderson, R. C., E. H. Hiebert, J. A. Scott, and I. A. G. Wilkinson. 1985. *Becoming a Nation of Readers: The Report of the Commission on Reading.* Washington, DC: The National Institute of Education.

Angelillo, J. 2003. *Writing About Reading: From Book Talk to Literary Essays, Grades 3–8.* Portsmouth, NH: Heinemann.

Bamford, R. A., and J. V. Kristo. 2003. *Making Facts Come Alive: Choosing & Using Nonfiction Literature K–8,* 2nd ed. Norwood, MA: Christopher-Gordon.

Banks, J. A. 2002. *An Introduction to Multicultural Education,* 3rd ed. Boston: Allyn & Bacon.

Barton, J. 2001. *Teaching with Children's Literature.* Norwood, MA: Christopher-Gordon.

Beaty, J. J. 1994. *Picture Book Storytelling: Literature Activities for Young Children.* Fort Worth, TX: Harcourt Brace College.

Berger, E. H. 2004. *Parents as Partners in Education,* 6th ed. Upper Saddle River, NJ: Merrill/Prentice Hall.

Block, C. C., and J. A. Zinke. 1995. *Creating a Culturally Enriched Curriculum for Grades K–6.* Boston: Allyn & Bacon.

Boyd, F. B., and C. H. Brock, with M. S. Rosendal, eds. 2004. *Multicultural and Multilingual Literacy and Language: Contexts and Practices.* New York: Guilford.

Bromley, K., and V. J. Risko. 2001 "Collaboration for Diverse Learners: Reflections and Recommendations." In *Collaboration for Diverse Learners: Viewpoints and Practices,* edited by V. J. Risko and K. Bromley, pp. 393–407. Newark, DE: International Reading Association.

Brown, H., and B. Cambourne. 1990. *Read and Retell: A Strategy for the Whole Language/Natural Learning Classroom.* Portsmouth, NH: Heinemann.

Buss, K., and L. Karnowski. 2000. *Reading and Writing Literary Genres.* Newark, DE: International Reading Association.

Campbell, R. 2001. *Read-Alouds with Young Children.* Newark, DE: International Reading Association.

Cary, S. 2000. *Working with Second Language Learners: Answers to Teachers' Top Ten Questions.* Portsmouth, NH: Heinemann.

Children's Books: Awards and Prizes. 1996. New York: The Children's Book Council.

Cianciolo, P. J. 1997. *Picture Books for Children*, 4th ed. Chicago: American Library Association.

Crago, H. 1993. "Why Readers Read What Writers Write." *Children's Literature in Education* 24 (4): 277–89.

Cramer, E. H., and M. Castle, eds. 1994. *Fostering the Love of Reading: The Affective Domain in Reading Education*. Newark, DE: International Reading Association.

Crawford, K., G. Crowell, G. Kauffman, B. Peterson, L. Phillips, J. Schroeder, C. Giorgis, and K. G. Short. 1994. "Finding Ourselves as People and as Learners." *The Reading Teacher* 48: 64–74.

Cullinan, B. E., ed. 1993a. *Children's Voices: Talk in the Classroom*. Newark, DE: International Reading Association.

———. 1993b. *Fact and Fiction: Literature Across the Curriculum*. Newark, DE: International Reading Association.

———. 1992. *Invitation to Read: More Children's Literature in the Reading Program*. Newark, DE: International Reading Association.

Daisey, P. 1993. "Three Ways to Promote the Values and Uses of Literacy at Any Age." *Journal of Reading* 36: 436–40.

Day, J. P., D. L. Spiegel, J. McLellan, and V. B. Brown. 2002. *Moving Forward with Literature Circles*. New York: Scholastic.

DeBruin-Parecki, A., and B. Krol-Sinclair. 2003. *Family Literacy: From Theory to Practice*. Newark, DE: International Reading Association.

Díaz-Rico, L. T., and K. Z. Weed. 2006. *The Crosscultural, Language, and Academic Development Handbook: A Complete K–12 Reference Guide*, 3rd ed. Boston: Allyn & Bacon.

Fader, D. N., and E. B. McNeil. 1968. *Hooked on Books: Programs and Proof*. New York: G. P. Putnam's Sons.

Farris, P. J. 2001. *Language Arts: Process, Product, and Assessment*, 3rd ed. Boston: McGraw-Hill.

Fennessey, S. 1995. "Living History through Drama and Literature." *The Reading Teacher* 49 (1): 16–19.

Flippo, R. F. 2004. *Texts and Tests: Teaching Study Skills Across Content Areas*. Portsmouth, NH: Heinemann.

———. 2003. *Assessing Readers: Qualitative Diagnosis and Instruction*. Portsmouth, NH: Heinemann.

———. ed. 2001. *Reading Researchers in Search of Common Ground*. Newark, DE: International Reading Association.

———. 1999. *What Do the Experts Say? Helping Children Learn to Read*. Portsmouth, NH: Heinemann.

———. 1998. "Points of Agreement: A Display of Professional Unity in Our Field." *The Reading Teacher* 52: 30–40.

———. 1982. *How to Help Grow a Reader*. Atlanta, GA: Metro Atlanta/Georgia State University Chapter Phi Delta Kappa.

Flippo, R. F., C. Hetzel, D. Gribouski, and L. A. Armstrong. 1997. "Creating a Student Literacy Corps in a Diverse Community." *Phi Delta Kappan* 78 (8): 644–46.

Flippo, R. F., and J. A. Smith. 1990. "Encouraging Parent Involvement Through Home Letters." *The Reading Teacher* 44 (4): 359.

Fountas, I. C., and G. S. Pinnell. 1999. *Matching Books to Readers: Using Leveled Books in Guided Reading, K–3.* Portsmouth, NH: Heinemann.

Fox, M. G. 1993. "Politics and Literature: Chasing the 'Isms' from Children's Books." *The Reading Teacher* 46: 654–58.

Fox, D. L., and K. G. Short, eds. 2003. *Stories Matter: The Complexity of Cultural Authenticity in Children's Literature.* Urbana, IL: National Council of Teachers of English.

France, M. G., and J. M. Hager. 1993. "Recruit, Respect, Respond: A Model for Working with Low-Income Families and Their Preschoolers." *The Reading Teacher* 46: 568–72.

Freeman, E. B., and D. G. Person. 1998. *Connecting Informational Children's Books with Content Area Learning.* Boston: Allyn & Bacon.

Freeman, E. B., and D. G. Person, eds. 1992. *Using Nonfiction Trade Books in the Elementary Classroom: From Ants to Zeppelins.* Urbana, IL: National Council of Teachers of English.

Friedberg, J. G., J. B. Mullins, and A. W. Sukiennik. 1992. *Portraying Persons with Disabilities: An Annotated Bibliography of Nonfiction for Children and Teenagers.* New Providence, NJ: R. R. Bowker.

Galda, L., and B. E. Cullinan. 2006. *Literature and the Child,* 6th ed. Belmont, CA: Wadsworth/Thomson Learning.

Galda, L., and J. West. 1995. "Exploring Literature Through Drama." In *Book Talk and Beyond: Children and Teachers Respond to Literature,* edited by N. L. Roser and M. G. Martinez, pp. 183–90. Newark, DE: International Reading Association.

———. 1992. "Enriching Our Lives: The Humanities in Children's Literature." *The Reading Teacher* 45: 536–45.

Gambrell, L. B. 2001. "What We Know About Motivation to Read." In *Reading Researchers in Search of Common Ground,* edited by R. F. Flippo, pp. 129–43. Newark, DE: International Reading Association.

Gersten, R., and R. T. Jiménez. 1994. "A Delicate Balance: Enhancing Literature Instruction for Students of English as a Second Language." *The Reading Teacher* 47: 438–49.

Gillespie, C. S., J. L. Powell, N. E. Clements, and R. A. Swearingen. 1994. "A Look at the Newbery Medal Books from a Multicultural Perspective." *The Reading Teacher* 48 (1): 40–50.

Glazer, J. I., and C. Giorgis. 2005. *Literature for Young Children,* 5th ed. Upper Saddle River, NJ: Merrill/Prentice Hall.

Gonzalez-Mena, J. 2005. *Diversity in Early Care and Education: Honoring Differences,* 4th ed. Boston: McGraw-Hill.

Goodman, Y. M., and M. M. Haussler. 1986. "Literacy Environment in the Home and Community." In *Roles in Literacy Learning,* edited by D. R. Tovey and J. E. Kerber, pp. 26–32. Newark, DE: International Reading Association.

Goodman, Y. M., D. J. Watson, and C. L. Burke. 1987. *Reading Miscue Inventory: Alternative Procedures.* Katonah, NY: Richard C. Owen.

Guthrie, J. T. 1994. "Creating Interest in Reading." *Reading Today* 12 (1): 24.

Guthrie, J. T., and A. Wigfield, eds. 1997. *Reading Engagement: Motivating Reading Through Integrated Instruction.* Newark, DE: International Reading Association.

Hancock, M. R. 2004. *A Celebration of Literature and Response,* 2nd ed. Upper Saddle River, NJ: Merrill/Prentice Hall.

Hancock, M. R. 1993. "Exploring and Extending Personal Response Through Literature Journals." *The Reading Teacher* 46 (6): 466–74.

Handloff, E., and J. M. Golden. 1995. "Writing as a Way of 'Getting to' What You Think and Feel About a Story." In *Book Talk and Beyond: Children and Teachers Respond to Literature,* edited by N. L. Roser and M. G. Martinez, pp. 201–07. Newark, DE: International Reading Association.

Hansen-Krening, N., E. M. Aoki, and D. T. Mizokawa, eds., and the Committee to Revise the Multicultural Booklist. 2003. *Kaleidoscope: A Multicultural Booklist for Grades K–8,* 4th ed. Urbana, IL: National Council of Teachers of English.

Harris, V. J., ed. 1997. *Using Multiethnic Literature in the Grades K–8 Classroom.* Norwood, MA: Christopher-Gordon.

Hayden, C. D., ed. 1992. *Venture into Cultures: A Resource Book of Multicultural Materials and Programs.* Chicago: American Library Association.

Henk, W. A., and S. A. Melnick. 1995. "The Reader Self-Perception Scale (RSPS): A New Tool for Measuring How Children Feel About Themselves as Readers." *The Reading Teacher* 48 (6): 470–82.

Hennings, D. G. 2002. *Communication in Action: Teaching Literature-Based Language Arts,* 8th ed. Boston: Houghton Mifflin.

Hill, B. C., K. L. S. Noe, and N. J. Johnson. 2001. *Literature Circles Resource Guide.* Norwood, MA: Christopher-Gordon.

Hoffman, J. V., N. L. Roser, and J. Battle. 1993. "Reading Aloud in the Classroom: From the Modal to a 'Model.'" *The Reading Teacher* 46: 496–503.

Huck, C. S., B. Kiefer, S. Hepler, and J. Hickman. 2004. *Children's Literature in the Elementary School,* 8th ed. Boston: McGraw-Hill.

Hunt, P. 1991. *Criticism, Theory and Children's Literature.* Cambridge, MA: Basil Blackwell.

International Reading Association. 1994. *Teachers' Favorite Books for Kids.* Newark, DE: International Reading Association.

International Reading Association and Children's Book Council. 1995. *More Kids' Favorite Books.* Newark, DE: International Reading Association.

———. 1992. *Kids' Favorite Books: Children's Choices 1989–1991.* Newark, DE: International Reading Association.

Jacobs, J. S., and M. O. Tunnell. 2004. *Children's Literature, Briefly,* 3rd ed. Upper Saddle River, NJ: Merrill/Prentice Hall.

Kletzien, S. B., and M. J. Dreher. 2004. *Informational Text in K–3 Classrooms: Helping Children Read and Write.* Newark, DE: International Reading Association.

Krashen, S. D. 2004. *The Power of Reading: Insights from the Research,* 2nd ed. Westport, CT: Libraries Unlimited/Greenwood Heinemann.

Kristo, J. V., and R. A. Bamford. 2004. *Nonfiction in Focus.* New York: Scholastic.

Kurkjian, C., N. Livingston, K. Henkes, R. Sabuda, and L. Yee. 2005. "Evocative Books: Books That Inspire Personal Response and Engagement." *The Reading Teacher* 58 (5): 480–88.

Leal, D. J. 1993. "The Power of Literacy Peer Group Discussions: How Children Collaboratively Negotiate Meaning." *The Reading Teacher* 47: 114–20.

Lewis, M. 1996. *Using Student-Centered Methods with Teacher-Centered ESL Students.* Portsmouth, NH: Pippin/Heinemann.

Lilly, E., and C. Green. 2004. *Developing Partnerships with Families Through Children's Literature.* Upper Saddle River, NJ: Merrill/Prentice Hall.

Lukens, R. J. 2003. *A Critical Handbook of Children's Literature*, 7th ed. Boston: Allyn & Bacon.

Many, J. E., D. L. Wiseman, and J. L. Altieri. 1996. "Exploring the Influences of Literature Approaches on Children's Stance When Responding and Their Response Complexity." *Reading Psychology* 17 (1): 1–41.

McGill-Franzen, A. 1993. "'I Could Read the Words!': Selecting Good Books for Inexperienced Readers." *The Reading Teacher* 46: 424–26.

McKenna, M. C., and D. J. Kear. 1990. "Measuring Attitude Toward Reading: A New Tool for Teachers." *The Reading Teacher* 43 (9): 626–39.

Miller-Lachmann, L. 1995. *Global Voices, Global Visions: A Core Collection of Multicultural Books.* New Providence, NJ: R. R. Bowker.

———. 1992. *Our Family Our Friends Our World: An Annotated Guide to Significant Multicultural Books for Children and Teenagers.* New Providence, NJ: R. R. Bowker.

Morrow, L. M., ed. 1995. *Family Literacy: Connections in Schools and Communities.* Newark, DE: International Reading Association.

Morrow, L. M., and E. A. Sharkey. 1993. "Motivating Independent Reading and Writing in the Primary Grades Through Social Cooperative Literary Experiences." *The Reading Teacher* 47: 162–65.

Morrow, L. M., D. H. Tracey, and C. M. Maxwell, eds. 1995. *A Survey of Family Literacy in the United States.* Newark, DE: International Reading Association.

Murrill, L. 2005. "Do Young Readers Need Happy Endings." In *Exploring Culturally Diverse Literature for Children and Adolescents*, edited by D. L. Henderson and J. P. May, pp. 356–68. Boston: Allyn & Bacon.

Nash, M. F. 1995. "'Leading from Behind': Dialogue Response Journals." In *Book Talk and Beyond: Children and Teachers Respond to Literature*, edited by N. L. Roser and M. G. Martinez, pp. 217–25. Newark, DE: International Reading Association.

Nieto, S. 2004. *Affirming Diversity: The Sociopolitical Context of Multicultural Education*, 4th ed. Boston: Allyn & Bacon.

Norton, D. E. 2005. *Multicultural Children's Literature: Through the Eyes of Many Children*, 2nd ed. Upper Saddle River, NJ: Merrill/Prentice Hall.

Norton, D. E., and S. Norton. 2003. *Through the Eyes of a Child: An Introduction to Children's Literature*, 6th ed. Upper Saddle River, NJ: Merrill/Prentice Hall.

Opitz, M. F., ed. 1998. *Literacy Instruction for Culturally and Linguistically Diverse Students.* Newark, DE: International Reading Association.

Opitz, M. F., and M. P. Ford. 2001. *Reaching Readers: Flexible & Innovative Strategies for Guided Reading.* Portsmouth, NH: Heinemann.

Ouzts, D. T. 1994. "Bibliotherapeutic Literature: A Key Facet of Whole Language Instruction for the At-Risk Student." *Reading Horizons* 35 (2): 161–75.

Pang, V. O. 2005. *Multicultural Education: A Caring-Centered, Reflective Approach.* Boston: McGraw-Hill.

Paratore, J. R., and R. L. McCormack, eds. 1997. *Peer Talk in the Classroom: Learning from Research.* Newark, DE: International Reading Association.

Post, A. D., with M. Scott and M. Theberge. 2000. *Celebrating Children's Choices: 25 Years of Children's Favorite Books.* Newark, DE: International Reading Association.

Pressley, M., S. E. Dolezal, L. M. Raphael, L. Mohan, A. D. Roehrig, and K. Bogner. 2003. *Motivating Primary-Grade Students.* New York: Guilford.

Prill, P. 1994/1995. "Helping Children Use the Classroom Library." *The Reading Teacher* 48: 365.

Rasinski, T. V., ed. 1995. *Parents and Teachers: Helping Children Learn to Read and Write.* Fort Worth, TX: Harcourt Brace College.

Rasinski, T. V., and C. S. Gillespie. 1992. *Sensitive Issues: An Annotated Guide to Children's Literature K–6.* Phoenix, AZ: Oryx Press.

Rasinski, T. V., and N. D. Padak. 2001. *From Phonics to Fluency: Effective Teaching of Decoding and Reading Fluency in the Elementary School.* New York: Addison Wesley Longman.

Rickards, D., and S. Hawes. 2005. *Learning About Literary Genres: Reading and Writing with Young Children.* Norwood, MA: Christopher-Gordon.

Risko, V. J., and K. Bromley, eds. 2001. *Collaboration for Diverse Learners: Viewpoints and Practices.* Newark, DE: International Reading Association.

Robertson, D. 1992. *Portraying Persons with Disabilities: An Annotated Bibliography of Fiction for Children and Teenagers,* 3rd ed. New Providence, NJ: R. R. Bowker.

Roginski, J., ed. 1992. *Newbery and Caldecott Medalists and Honor Book Winners.* New York: Neal-Schuman.

Rosenblatt, L. 1991. "Literature—S.O.S.!" *Language Arts* 68: 444–48.

———. 1989. "Writing and Reading: The Transactional Theory." In *Reading and Writing Connections,* edited by J. M. Mason, pp. 153–76. Boston: Allyn & Bacon.

———. 1985. "The Transactional Theory of the Literary Work." In *Researching Response to Literature and the Teaching of Literature,* edited by C. R. Cooper, pp. 33–53. Norwood, NJ: Ablex.

———. L. 1978. *The Reader, the Text, the Poem: The Transactional Theory of the Literary Work.* Carbondale, IL: Southern Illinois University Press.

Roser, N. L., and M. G. Martinez, eds. 1995. *Book Talk and Beyond: Children and Teachers Respond to Literature.* Newark, DE: International Reading Association.

Routman, R. 2000. *Conversations: Strategies for Teaching, Learning, and Evaluating*. Portsmouth, NH: Heinemann.

Rowe, R., and C. Probst. 1995. "Connecting with Local Culture." *Educational Leadership* 53 (1): 62–64.

Rudman, M. K. 1995. *Children's Literature: An Issues Approach*, 3rd ed. White Plains, NY: Longman.

Rudman, M. K., K. D. Gagne, and J. E. Bernstein. 1994. *Books to Help Children Cope with Separation and Loss*, 4th ed. New Providence, NJ: R. R. Bowker.

Russell, D. L. 2005. *Literature for Children: A Short Introduction*, 5th ed. Boston: Allyn & Bacon.

Saccardi, M. 1993/1994. "Children Speak: Our Students' Reactions to Books Can Tell Us What to Teach." *The Reading Teacher* 47: 318–24.

Samway, K. D., G. Whang, and M. Pippitt. 1995. *Buddy Reading: Cross-Age Tutoring in a Multicultural School*. Portsmouth, NH: Heinemann.

Schon, I., and C. Berkin. 1996. *Introducción a la Literatura Infantil y Juvenil*. Newark, DE: International Reading Association.

Scott, J. E. 1994. "Teaching Nonfiction with the Shared Book Experience." *The Reading Teacher* 47: 676–678.

Shockley, B. 1994. "Extending the Literature Community: Home-to-School and School-to-Home." *The Reading Teacher* 47: 500–02.

Shockley, B., B. Michalove, and J. Allen. 1995. *Engaging Families: Connecting Home and School Literacy Communities*. Portsmouth, NH: Heinemann.

Short, K. G., ed. 1995. *Research & Professional Resources in Children's Literature: Piecing a Patchwork Quilt*. Newark, DE: International Reading Association.

Simmons, J. S., ed. 1994. *Censorship: A Threat to Reading, Learning, Thinking*. Newark, DE: International Reading Association.

Slaughter, J. P. 1993. *Beyond Storybooks: Young Children and the Shared Book Experience*. Newark, DE: International Reading Association.

Stoll, D. R. ed. 1997. *Magazines for Kids and Teens*, rev. ed. Newark, DE: International Reading Association.

Stoodt-Hill, B. D., and L. B. Amspaugh-Corson. 2005. *Children's Literature: Discovery for a Lifetime*, 3rd ed. Upper Saddle River, NJ: Merrill/Prentice Hall.

Sullivan, J. 2004. *The Children's Literature Lover's Book of Lists*. San Francisco: Jossey-Bass/Wiley & Sons.

Sutherland, Z. 1997. *Children and Books*, 9th ed. Boston: Longman/Allyn & Bacon.

Swindal, D. N. 1993. "The Big Advantage: Using Big Books for Shared Reading Experiences in the Classroom." *The Reading Teacher* 46: 716–17.

Taylor, D., ed. 1997. *Many Families, Many Literacies: An International Declaration of Principles*. Portsmouth, NH: Heinemann.

Tiedt, P. L., and I. M. Tiedt. 2005. *Multicultural Teaching: A Handbook of Activities, Information, and Resources*, 7th ed. Boston: Allyn & Bacon.

Tompkins, G. E., and L. M. McGee. 1993. *Teaching Reading with Literature: Case Studies to Action Plans*. New York: Macmillan.

Trelease, J. 2001. *The Read-Aloud Handbook*, 5th ed. New York: Penguin.

———. 1992. *Hey! Listen to This: Stories to Read Aloud*. New York: Penguin.

Wilson, P. J., and R. F. Abrahamson. 1988. "What Children's Literature Classics Do Children Really Enjoy?" *The Reading Teacher* 41: 406–11.

Wlodkowski, R. J., and M. B. Ginsberg. 1995. "A Framework for Culturally Responsive Teaching." *Educational Leadership* 53 (1): 17–21.

Young, T. A., ed. 2004. *Happily Ever After: Sharing Folk Literature with Elementary and Middle School Students*. Newark, DE: International Reading Association.

Young, T. A., and S. Vardell. 1993. "Weaving Readers Theatre and Nonfiction into the Curriculum." *The Reading Teacher* 46: 396–06.

Zarrillo, J. 1994. *Multicultural Literature, Multicultural Teaching: Units for the Elementary Grades*. Fort Worth, TX: Harcourt Brace College.